The Next Steps
in Central America

Brookings Dialogues on Public Policy

The presentations and discussions at Brookings conferences and seminars often deserve wide circulation as contributions to public understanding of issues of national importance. The Brookings Dialogues on Public Policy series is intended to make such statements and commentary available to a broad and general audience, usually in summary form. The series supplements the Institution's research publications by reflecting the contrasting, often lively, and sometimes conflicting views of elected and appointed government officials, other leaders in public and private life, and scholars. In keeping with their origin and purpose, the Dialogues are not subjected to the formal review procedures established for the Institution's research publications. Brookings publishes them in the belief that they are worthy of public consideration but does not assume responsibility for their accuracy or objectivity. And, as in all Brookings publications, the judgments, conclusions, and recommendations presented in the Dialogues should not be ascribed to the trustees, officers, or other staff members of the Brookings Institution.

The Next Steps
in Central America

Edited by

BRUCE L. R. SMITH

Papers presented at a conference held in Washington, D.C.,

June 19–21, 1990, sponsored by the Brookings Institution and

the Instituto Centroamericano de Administracion de Empresas

THE BROOKINGS INSTITUTION / Washington, D.C.

Copyright © 1991 by
THE BROOKINGS INSTITUTION
1775 Massachusetts Avenue, N.W.
Washington, D.C. 20036

LIBRARY OF CONGRESS CATALOG CARD NUMBER 91-072866

ISBN 0-8157-5063-3

9 8 7 6 5 4 3 2 1

About Brookings

The Brookings Institution is a private nonprofit organization devoted to research, education, and publication in economics, government, foreign policy, and the social sciences generally. Its principal purpose is to bring knowledge to bear on the current and emerging public policy problems facing the American people. In its research, Brookings functions as an independent analyst and critic, committed to publishing its findings for the information of the public. In its conferences and other activities, it serves as a bridge between scholarship and public policy, bringing new knowledge to the attention of decisionmakers and affording scholars a better insight into policy issues. Its activities are carried out through three research programs (Economic Studies, Governmental Studies, Foreign Policy Studies), a Center for Public Policy Education, a Publications Program, and a Social Science Computation Center.

The Institution was incorporated in 1927 to merge the Institute for Government Research, founded in 1916 as the first private organization devoted to public policy issues at the national level; the Institute of Economics, established in 1922 to study economic problems; and the Robert Brookings Graduate School of Economics and Government, organized in 1924 as a pioneering experiment in training for public service. The consolidated institution was named in honor of Robert Somers Brookings (1850–1932), a St. Louis businessman whose leadership shaped the earlier organizations.

Brookings is financed largely by endowment and by the support of philanthropic foundations, corporations, and private individuals. Its funds are devoted to carrying out its own research and educational activities. It also undertakes some unclassified government contract studies, reserving the right to publish its findings.

A Board of Trustees is responsible for general supervision of the Institution, approval of fields of investigation, and safeguarding the independence of the Institution's work. The President is the chief administrative officer, responsible for formulating and coordinating policies, recommending projects, approving publications, and selecting staff.

Editor's Preface

The Brookings Institution's conference, The Next Steps in Central America, took place in June 1990, when important changes were occurring in the Spanish-speaking countries of Central America. Since then events have moved the region further along the path toward peaceful change. I hope the papers in this volume will contribute to the enlightened public debate that will bring the United States and its friends in the region closer together on the important choices for the future.

Many people played important roles in the collaborative effort between the Brookings Institution and the Instituto Centroamericano de Administracion de Empresas (INCAE). Louis W. Cabot, chairman of the board of trustees of the Brookings Institution, and his wife Maryellen took an active interest in the project from the start. Their enthusiasm and vision were indispensable. The contributions of Robert J. Kurz, visiting fellow in the Brookings Foreign Policy Studies program, were critical to the success of the conference. His good humor, energy, and knowledge of the region were invaluable. Melvyn R. Copen, president of INCAE, and Roger Quant, of INCAE's senior staff, also contributed greatly to the conference.

Brookings gratefully acknowledges the financial support provided by the following institutions: the Cabot Family Charitable Trust, the Foundation for Management Education in Central America, and the Inter-American Foundation.

Bruce L. R. Smith

July 1991
Washington, D.C.

Contents

BRUCE L. R. SMITH

A Transformation in Central America?

The year 1989 witnessed a dramatic transformation in the world's political landscape, particularly in the events in Germany, the Soviet
Union, and the nations of Central and Eastern Europe. Policymakers
and pundits have been preoccupied with the implications of these
great events, notwithstanding the more recent Gulf crisis and talk of
a New World Order. Closer to home, and almost overlooked in the
process, are the equally profound developments in Central America.
The initiative of the Bush administration in the foreign policy arena
served, first, to forge a bipartisan agreement with the Democratic
leadership in Congress to end the rancorous disputes over Central
American policy that had marked the Reagan era. Meanwhile, partly
in response to their own internal logic, as well as to the U.S. policy
initiatives, events in Central America began to take a different turn.
The stunning upset victory of Violeta Barrios de Chamorro and her
opposition coalition in the Nicaraguan elections of February 1989—
and, significantly, the acquiescence by the Sandinistas in the election
result—most dramatically marked the turnaround in Central America.

In the face of the triumph of democracy in Nicaragua, the ouster of
Noriega from power in Panama, and the apparent slowdown in military activity by the insurgents in El Salvador, the region appeared to
be on the brink of a new epoch. Democracy, privatization of the economy, and regional peace seemed to be within reach. Astounding as
they were, these events faded all too quickly from public attention in
the United States as they were eclipsed by the transformation in Eastern Europe. While the American people were still celebrating the
triumph of peace and democracy in Europe, the inevitable return to a
more sober reality, if not quite to disillusionment, began to set in
among observers of Central America.

In this context, in the spring of 1990, the Brookings Institution decided that the time was ripe to scrutinize the developments in Central America and to assess the next steps for this important region. Now that the domestic political conflicts that had so envenomed the policy debate seemed at an end, what steps should the United States now take in its policy toward the region? This question inevitably merged into the broad issues of the appropriate roles of multilateral institutions, the Central American nations themselves, possible regional institutions, and bilateral aid both to promote economic development and to foster the progress toward democratic institution-building. Stable progress toward democracy and market economies promised that the continuing civil wars could be resolved and that a stable regional peace could be achieved.

We sought the assistance of the Instituto Centroamericano de Administracion de Empresas (INCAE) in planning a conference that could bring together policymakers and scholarly observers from the United States and Central America to address the region's emerging political, economic, and military issues. This conference was held at Brookings in June 1990 for two and a half days. The conference, in our view, successfully identified and clarified the major policy options that must be faced in the next phase of Central America's development. The present volume seeks to advance the most important next steps by presenting the papers, edited and in some cases revised by their authors in the light of the conference discussions, that were prepared for the seminar. This introductory essay attempts to link the analytical themes of the papers into a whole, and to provide a few highlights of the debates that were generated among the conference participants by the authors' presentations.

STABLE DEMOCRATIC INSTITUTIONS IN CENTRAL AMERICA

The conference organizers from INCAE and Brookings considered the following themes of particular importance—the prospects for democracy in the region, the drive toward privatization and market economies in the context of new strategies for economic development, and the achievement of internal peace and regional security within a framework that would reduce the power traditionally enjoyed by military elites. These three areas are, of course, interrelated in complex and subtle ways—poverty breeding unrest, authoritarianism blocking the development of free markets, economic monopolies impeding political pluralism, and civil disorder weakening the rule of law. Yet, the priority seemed to rest clearly with the transition to democracy in the region. Two papers, by Mark Rosenberg of Florida International University and Sergio Julio Ramirez of INCAE, analyze the transition to democratic institutions, assess the progress made to date, and recommend ways to strengthen and consolidate the process of democratization. The papers succeeded admirably in presenting critical issues and sparked some of the most illuminating discussions at the conference.

Rosenberg and Ramirez both take as their point of departure the striking reversals that occurred during the decade of the 1980s. At the beginning of the decade, only Costa Rica of the six Spanish-speaking Central American countries was a stable democracy. From April 25, 1990, all six had civilian governments that had assumed power as the result of free elections for the first time in their collective history. In Nicaragua, as Ramirez points out, for the first time since the formation of the republic more than 150 years before, a peaceful transition of power through democratic elections had occurred. The opposition gained power, and the incumbent government was willing to step down (at least from control of the highest office). The 1989 transfer of power in El Salvador was the first between government and opposition as the result of an election since 1931. In Guatemala, after several decades of power transfers via military coup, a government gained power through free and fair elections; in January 1991 new presidential elections were held that resulted in the election of the first non-Catholic, Jorge Serrano Elias, as president of a Latin American country. Not all political factions competed in the election, however, and guerrilla activity continued to circumscribe progress toward full democracy. Competitive and open elections leading to a peaceful change of power also took place in Honduras for the first time in thirty years. In Panama constitutional government returned to power after U.S. military action destroyed the regime of General Manuel Noriega. All of this was a remarkable achievement, the more so because it occurred in poor countries, unaided by nationalist overtones of deposing regimes installed by a foreign power, and, in several cases, in the midst of civil strife.

Both papers make the point, approaching the matter from slightly different perspectives, that the transition to democracy will not mean domestic tranquillity and harmony. In fact, democratic rule will presage more noisy, clamorous, and, on the surface, unstable conditions as new groups, political alignments, and social forces compete for power and influence. Both authors, as well as the conference participants, clearly sensed that the region's troubles would not end with the advent of the first stages of democracy. Indeed, the more formidable challenges lay ahead and, in recognition of this fact, there was little of the euphoria that accompanied the swift demise of communist rule in Eastern Europe. By the same token, one could judge from the reactions of the Central American participants that they would also be spared the disillusionment that was the inevitable concomitant of the euphoria that swept Central and Eastern Europe.

While agreeing on the general diagnosis and the cautionary note that consolidating democratic rule would be an even greater challenge than the initial transition, Rosenberg and Ramirez diverge somewhat in their prescriptions of what should happen next. Rosenberg emphasizes the traditional weaknesses of legislative institutions in Central and Latin America; he urges a strategy that would improve the internal institutions of government, especially the legislative and judicial branches, as priority concerns. Ramirez appears to focus more on devices to enhance popular participation in government; he attributes the weaknesses of Central American democracy to an overly powerful state with only very shallow roots in the societies at large. The solution, in his view, is to employ plebescitarian devices to "jump start" the democratic process. Votes, plebescites, opinion surveys, mass media techniques—whatever gives the citizen a sense of identification with government—could serve to instill deeper habits of participation and attitudes broadly supportive of democracy.

A somewhat more controversial note is the notion of "consociational" or power-sharing arrangements to avert conflict in situations of intense social tension or potential civil strife. The idea here, as developed only briefly by Ramirez from the literature of comparative politics, is that, for a transitional period, majority rule might be modified or replaced by agreements among groups to exclude key social issues from the normal tug and pull of politics. Implicit in this view is a belief that democracy guarantees outcomes and not merely a process—a device to be employed only sparingly and only when tensions are sufficiently great that they doom the normal workings of political competition. Ramirez seems unwilling to push the idea too far, noting that "consociational practices . . . should not be expected to last forever, if the purpose is to democratize the political system." Such arrangements, moreover, may not always succeed in averting conflict if the demands and desired outcomes of a group are considered too extreme to be accommodated by the others.

Rosenberg and Ramirez, as well as most conference participants, could agree in principle that the size and political weight of military bureaucracies was a danger to the long-term stability and the survival of democracy in Central America. Smaller military forces would not only promote democracy but also free revenues for economic development. But the near-term problem of the continuing civil war in El Salvador, with its potential ramifications for instability in Nicaragua and elsewhere, confronted the conference participants with a dilemma. Continued civil disorder would threaten the rule of law, democratic political competition, and economic prosperity. To the extent that insurgent groups threatened violence as the principal political tactic to achieve their ends (or embraced the struggle itself as the end), the Salvadoran government would be forced to maintain a strong military presence. The presence of continued armed conflict differentiated, and complicated, the Central American as compared with the situation in Central and Eastern Europe where domestic peace largely prevailed. Nevertheless, the tortuous movement toward a negotiated settlement of the conflict gave an air of hope—almost palpable at times—to the conference.

One poignant moment reflecting this spirit came as General Adolfo Blandon, defense attaché from El Salvador and former army chief of staff, rose to address the conferees. He observed that, although he and Ruben Zamora, general secretary of the Popular Social Christian Movement, grew up together in the same village, they had not spoken for twenty years; he found Zamora's earlier remarks very thoughtful and constructive, and he hoped that Zamora might find something of value in his comments.

The ending of the cold war in Europe was also discussed in this context. The conferees generally concluded as an analytical observation but one also tinged with hope, that the easing of cold war tensions would result in the reduction of outside resources for the support of either insurgency or counterinsurgency. As the civil war came to be a matter of extracting more resources from the country itself and the region at the cost of resources and energies available for social and economic infrastructure, the prospects for winding down, settling, or simply abandoning the conflict through exhaustion seemed brighter. To some North American participants, it appeared a paradoxical outcome that the United States might accomplish through neglect what it could not achieve through massive security assistance.

Looking to the future, the consolidation of democracy in Central America still left a host of thorny conceptual and practical difficulties. Where would the expertise come from to assist the Central American countries in reforming their legal systems? Experts from the United States and Europe knowledgeable enough in this area to be truly useful were, and are, in notoriously short supply.

The future of the civil service in Central America came in for extended and fascinating commentary. Caudillism, personalism, and fractionalism have tended to weaken the effectiveness of bureaucratic institutions. The democratic representation of interests, citizen access to authority, and leadership formation have been difficult in systems accustomed to elite and extralegal manipulation. The statism or strong executive authority thought to characterize Central America has evidently been something of a hollow shell. As economic opportunity develops, the incentives diminish for enterprising officials to remain in public service at low salaries. Paradoxically, a consensus seemed to develop that a strengthened and more effective public service was a precondition for rapid progress toward freeing the economy from unnecessary and restrictive controls.

At a more profound level, the discussion of ways in which to strengthen democracy in Central America frequently returned to the underlying issue of whether the Westminster model of the United Kingdom, the separation of powers system of the United States, the Costa Rica model, or some unique variant of their own, should be the model for which the five new Central American democracies should strive. Equally difficult was determining which stage of democratic development should be the goal—an early twentieth century version stressing the role of competing oligarchical political parties; the 1950s democracy of the United States with significant minorities excluded from effective participation; or the "full" or mature democratic practices featuring media manipulation, PACs, incumbent domination of elections, and PR systems that might splinter the electorate? Asking these questions begins the process of understanding the complexity of the challenge. Democracy, in the five nations other than Costa Rica, was not yet irreversibly implanted, and the broader sense of citizenship that nurtures and sustains the habits of political accommodation has yet to take firm root. Because the participants from Central America considered the task without facile optimism and self-deception, however, this observer emerged with a strong sense of confidence and hope for the future. A "creeping democratization" is apparently occurring that is moving Central America inexorably away from its past.

STRATEGIES FOR ECONOMIC DEVELOPMENT

The dismal decade in economic terms for Latin America needs no elaborate commentary here. As Margaret Daly Hayes points out in her contribution to this volume, the facts are even harsher for Central America than for the hemisphere as a whole. While investment, for example, declined from approximately 24 to 16 percent of GDP for all of Latin America during the 1980s, it fell more sharply in every Central American country except Costa Rica (where it also declined from 30 to 23 percent of GDP). Foreign investment, following the slowing pattern of domestic investment, by the end of the decade had nearly abandoned Central America.

Population growth, meanwhile, continued at nearly 3 percent per annum despite substantial out-migration. The predictable result of the interrelated economic and demographic trends was decline in per capita growth rates and per capita income. For Latin America as a whole, per capita growth was down 8 percent over the 1982–89 period. Per capita GDP shares for Central America, during the decade of the 1980s, fell by 17 percent—roughly twice the drop suffered by Latin America as a whole (Costa Rica fell by 6 percent, Honduras by 12 percent, El Salvador, Panama, and Guatemala by 17 percent, and war-wracked Nicaragua by 33 percent). Unemployment and underemployment increased to record levels throughout the region, while poverty, malnutrition, and inequality were exacerbated.

The Brookings-INCAE conference took place at a time when a series of favorable signs began to create new hope for an economic turnaround. As the military activity wound down and as political stability returned, economic planners as well as entrepreneurs in the region focused their energies on strategies for growth. Central themes that emerge in the papers by Hayes and by Juan Vicente Maldonado, and that formed the basis for much of the economic discussion at the conference, concern the need to revive the private sectors in the Central American nations, to reverse the inward-looking and autarchic tendencies that contributed to the economic slowdown, and to rationalize the pattern of multilateral and bilateral economic assistance to the region.

Both Hayes and Maldonado begin their analyses with the recognition that market economics open to the world economy offer the best hope of promoting growth in Central America as in the nations of Eastern Europe. They eschew any effort to find a "middle way" between central planning and market economics. Nowhere has such a strategy proved workable. But for Central America the task seems both easier and more difficult than for the formerly communist nations of Eastern Europe. Aside from the overt Marxism of the Sandinista regime and the former (abandoned as of March 1991) Marxist ideological leanings of the Farabundo Marti National Liberation Front (FMLN) in El Salvador, the institutions of private property have been nominally present. The private sectors in Costa Rica, Panama, and El Salvador, and even in Guatemala and Honduras, have remained in existence. It is not a question of creating something wholly new but of reactivating, in the varied circumstances of the countries, the energies of entrepreneurs and relearning the disciplines of the marketplace. The problem has been that politics have dominated economic decisionmaking, and cozy arrangements between political and economic elites have substituted for the rigorous disciplines of the marketplace.

The public sectors also grew in size and weight in the economy, sometimes as part of "reforms" produced by economic aid packages. Privatizing the economies, reducing the weight of the public sector, and creating genuinely competitive conditions instead of the dominance of a few powerful firms will be major challenges everywhere. Nicaragua poses special problems. The private sector in Nicaragua has been the most seriously affected and was nearly destroyed by the years of Sandinista rule. The situation in El Salvador, analyzed well in the Maldonado paper, calls for less dramatic remedies but reflects the problems of state-sanctioned monopolies and limited competition.

Panama's private sector was never totally suppressed even at the height of Noriega's power and appears to be in a better position to recover its vitality.

The steps outlined in the papers, and strongly endorsed by many of the participants, actually seem to have been undertaken—at least in some measure—in the period since the conference. Even in Nicaragua, Violeta de Chamorro's government has made progress toward privatization, marked by a significant new initiative in March 1991 to accelerate the process of long-term reform and to move toward short-term stabilization in her economic policies. Whether foreign direct investment has followed or will follow the gradual steps toward liberalization is difficult to assess at this time.

Apart from domestic economic reform, the conference participants devoted major attention to issues of regional integration and of economic assistance. A consensus among the conferees on these points was difficult to discern, but the discussions seemed to run along two tracks. One tended to stress the need to improve the framework for economic assistance both on the supply (that is, donor) side and on the demand (that is, recipient) side. While not necessarily agreeing that the levels of multilateral and bilateral assistance were adequate to the development needs, some participants believed that aid could be substantially more effective if the recipient nations were better organized internally and as a region to identify their needs and to channel resources to the appropriate targets. There appeared to be a general sense that more regional coordination was required. The discussions seemed almost to anticipate the notion of the Regional Consultation Group (RCG) that emerged from the Puntarenas Summit Declaration of December 17, 1990. The Summit Declaration of the Central American presidents urged the Inter-American Development Bank (IDB) to coordinate such a group, and, as of spring 1991, the IDB was scheduled to discuss plans for the new group at its April Board of Governors meeting. The Regional Consultative Group would be modeled after the individual groups for each country organized several years ago under the auspices of the World Bank.

A regional common market is suggested in the Hayes paper as part of the effort to emerge from inward-looking economic policies that prevailed during the decade of the 1980s. This idea stimulated a lively discussion at the conference, stirring some participants to query whether this step would be an anachronism in light of the goal of integrating Central America more fully into the world economy. In what sense could the limited Central American market be used to stimulate economic activity and trade? How could the Central American countries in practical terms coordinate macroeconomic policies when their debt situations, inflation rates, and domestic savings differed? Did one envisage a customs union along the lines of the Treaty of Rome?

No definitive answers to such questions emerged, but the proponents considered the revival of the once vigorous Central American common market as an effort to proceed in stages toward full integration into the international economy—and into whatever regional trading arrangement might emerge between North and South America. In the 1960s and 1970s intraregional trade flourished, and revival of the common market might serve to stimulate trade and regional economic competitiveness. It was agreed that trade among these poor and deficit-ridden countries alone could not substitute for the expansion of exports beyond Central America itself. The conference debated ways that the region could fit into the broader framework of U.S. and multilateral donor policies toward Latin America as a whole.

In several respects, the discussion again anticipated some of the subsequent debate over the proposed U.S.-Mexico trade pact and other hemisphere-wide economic issues. The government of Mexico has, since the beginning of 1991, assumed the responsibility of working with the Central American nations to promote trade expansion between the region and Mexico. The prospect has been held open for Central America, once it has undertaken appropriate economic reforms, to be included by the middle of the decade in the prospective free trade agreement between the United States and Mexico (and possibly Chile).

The second broad viewpoint that surfaced in the conference discussions of the economic papers was that internal economic reform, greater regional coordination, and improved donor cooperation could all play some useful role. But the participants sharing this orientation attached greater significance to the levels, not the modalities, of economic assistance. They considered the economic problems of the region profound and deep-rooted, subject largely to shocks over which the countries had little control, and less amenable to short-term improvements than the reformers might assume. According to their view, the important factors were stable, long-term commitments to economic assistance from the developed world and international agencies, and even increased aid levels to help compensate for the devastation wrought by the past decade's war-induced disruptions and turmoil. It is estimated, for example, that approximately 2.5 million people, or about 10 percent of the total population of the region, have been displaced from their homes.

In particular, any sharp reduction in U.S. aid was thought to be potentially disastrous for such objectives as continuation of the economic and political reforms and the achievement of a secure peace. There was considerable apprehension that the end of the cold war might lead to a loss of interest in the region and to reduced levels of U.S. support.

During the 1980s the United States was by far the largest supplier of aid to Central America. Support from Europe, Japan, and international institutions was limited, although the Soviet Union gave considerable military and economic assistance to Nicaragua. U.S. assistance to Central America began to expand significantly in the early 1980s as relations with the Sandinista government deteriorated and the insurgency in El Salvador intensified. U.S. aid increased to about $600 million in 1984 and then jumped to $1.6 billion in 1985 after the Kissinger Commission on Central America had urged a massive increase to combat the crisis confronting the region. U.S. aid subsequently stabilized at around $1 billion a year, excluding the special appropriation in 1990 of $720 million earmarked for Panama and Nicaragua in the wake of General Noriega's ouster and the electoral defeat of the Sandinistas. No argument was made that this aid was always well spent, but any sharp decline at this stage would be a source of instability and hardship for nations struggling to combat extreme poverty among nearly half of their populations and to generate foreign exchange for reigniting economic growth.

No one could be sure, then or now, of the "right" level of aid to promote recovery and restore long-term growth, because the economic outlook for the region was (and is) affected by numerous factors. Every Central American country is an oil importer, and a dollar increase in the price of a barrel of oil adds approximately $35 million a year to the region's oil import bill. Panama and Nicaragua are in arrears on their debt payments to the international lending institutions, and all but Costa Rica are in arrears to their commercial creditors, which limits access to new loans. Costa Rica, however, has benefited from substantial debt reduction from the United States under the Brady Plan, and Central America potentially could be the main beneficiary of the reductions in the U.S. bilateral debts proposed in June 1990 under President Bush's Enterprise for the Americas Initiative.

The prices of Central America's traditional exports have remained low, and efforts to stimulate nontraditional exports have so far shown only mixed results. Investment by multinational companies may or may not increase; and, if so, the net impact on job creation and growth in the region is uncertain. Rationalized production by the multinationals could merely displace small producers in the region. And, of course, continuing guerrilla activity causes instabilities and imposes social costs (for example, refugees continue to flow across borders to escape from the fighting). The United Nations Economic Commission for Latin America and the Caribbean summed up the economic outlook as of December 1990 as follows:

> In the midst of great difficulties, Latin America and the Caribbean are still trying to put a distinctive end to the crisis that has been overwhelming them for nearly a decade now. . . . In general, the countries of the Central American Common Market suffered a reduction in their growth rates as a result of the fall in the prices of their export products and the negative impact of the oil price rises. The exception was El Salvador, where the growth rate of the economy recovered to 3 percent thanks to the significant rise in agricultural production.[1]

A few benchmarks are available to indicate appropriate aid levels. In 1989, a blue-ribbon panel—the International Commission for Central American Recovery and Development (the Sanford Commission)—concluded that the five countries of Central America, excluding Panama, required $2 billion a year in external capital flows for a five-year period in addition to significant debt relief. The Kissinger Commission had reached similar conclusions approximately five years earlier. External assistance in significant amounts, by whatever estimate, seemed to be urgently needed in the view of most conference participants. Many also worried aloud that Latin America in general and Central America in particular might get lost in the shuffle as the world turned its attention to Central and Eastern Europe. The events in the Persian Gulf since then would only reinforce this fear:

1. United Nations Economic Commission on Latin America and the Caribbean (ECLA), *Preliminary Overview of the Economy of Latin America and the Caribbean 1990* (United Nations, 1990), pp. 1, 6.

scarce capital could be increasingly absorbed in the Middle East, where oil revenues are available to pay for reconstruction.

To reassure the countries of Central America, on November 20, 1990, the United States hosted a meeting to discuss the proposal for a Partnership for Democracy and Development in Central America (PDD). Invited to the meeting were government representatives from the twenty-four OECD countries, the six Central American countries, and Central America's closest neighbors, as well as representatives from international organizations. The purpose of the new partnership was, in a sense, to bridge the gap between those who placed the greatest stress on coordinating donor activity and those who sought increased assistance for the region. The proposal sought both improved coordination and increased aid levels.

The State Department Fact Sheet on PDD declared that the Washington meeting had produced broad agreement that

> An unprecedented and historic opportunity now exists for Central America to break out of its old patterns and move forward toward the goals set out in the Esquipulas process by its democratically elected governments: democratization, peace and demilitarization, respect for human rights, economic development, a Central American economic community, and more open market economies.

The Central American presidents, in their December 17, 1990, Puntarenas Summit Declaration expressed "satisfaction with the proposal to establish the Partnership for Democracy and Development in Central America, designed to create a forum to strengthen peace and democracy and to contribute to the economic development of Central America." Planning and staff work were under way to implement the proposal, and further discussions were scheduled in various forums. As of the date of this writing in spring 1991, however, the new partnership was a hope and not a reality.

DEMILITARIZATION AND REGIONAL SECURITY

At the root of numerous problems discussed at the conference were the complex issues of peace and security. It was recognized that the democratic reforms as well as economic development would be decisively influenced by the evolution of the military's role in society and the course of the conflicts that still raged. Without a full peace, the reduction of both military establishments and military budgets, and genuine regional security, none of the other goals could be achieved. Military considerations have been so pervasive that even Costa Rica, which dismantled its armed forces almost forty years ago, felt compelled to increase the size of its national police force during the 1980s.

Richard L. Millett's concluding chapter in this volume addresses this range of questions from a broad historical perspective. He demonstrates the way in which the military rose historically to the prominent position it enjoys in the Central American countries (again with the exception of Costa Rica). Of particular interest is his analysis of the recent trends that have witnessed a shift away from military intervention in civilian politics to intramilitary jockeying to the "civilianization" of the military in which military elites have been uncertain and divided about the limits of their own power. His paper set the stage for a frank and complex discussion.

In summary, the three conditions that were required are achieving an end to the fighting through a cease-fire, reducing the size and weight of military forces, and forging a regional scrutiny regime and a definitive peace treaty that would demobilize insurgent armies. The three conditions, in the view of most conferees, had somehow to be achieved more or less simultaneously or, at least, in close sequence. An end to the fighting was required before the size of military forces could be reduced, but an inducement to end the fighting would be the prospect of a society in which the social forces aligned with the military would not outweigh all the others. Although the fighting actively continued in only El Salvador and Honduras, other countries were involved as sanctuary and support for the fighters or suffered negative externalities as a result of the continued violence, or both. Before any one country could or would disarm, therefore, it would need assurances that others would abide by a disarmament regime, refrain from covert or overt aid to any insurrection, and cooperate to enhance the security of all (in, say, drug enforcement, where a national police force alone might be insufficient).

To achieve disarmament of insurgent groups might not, some feared, mean a definitive end to the fighting. Military action could cease, or gradually be reduced in scope and intensity, without full assurances against possible reignition of hostilities at a future point. Weapons were sufficiently available to make it difficult to certify demobilization. This would act as a check against full disarmament by the military. By the same token, how could a reduction in the size of the military be guaranteed? If armies nominally decreased in size but retained sizable reserve forces or retired units of some coherence, would this actually achieve the goal of reducing the weight and influence of the military?

Considerable discussion centered on the Salvadoran *tanda* system, which is the practice of military officers giving almost total support and protection to fellow officers from their class, or *tanda* of the military academy. Some conferees argued that a change in the training and education of the military, especially in El Salvador, but elsewhere as well, was a prerequisite to democratic reform. The almost total destruction of the former Panama Defense Force by the U.S. military solved the problem through drastic means in that country. By extension it was urged that further U.S. aid should be conditioned on radical reorganization and reform of the military forces in El Salvador and elsewhere.

Others strongly objected to this line of argument, insisting that the analysis was flawed and dramatically misrepresented the nature of the *tanda* system. The growing complexity of Central American societies seemed to question the simple image of societies dominated by an all-powerful military. The observation made by Richard Millett in his essay here with respect to Honduras, Guatemala, and El Salvador is highly pertinent in this connection:

> Although the military has expanded greatly in each nation during the past decade, the repeatedly predicted militarization of the societies may not be occurring. Military power has increased, and the concept of mission has expanded, but the relative institutional advantage that the armed forces have long held over other sectors of society has actually diminished. Political parties, labor groups, private-sector organizations, and religious bodies have developed ties that rival those of the military. At the same time, urbanization and the revolution in mass communications have made it impossible to exercise the degree of control over information, organization, and political action that was possible forty years ago.

The nature of a regional security arrangement prompted extended discussion. Unlike the situation in Europe, there were neither the remnants of a Warsaw Pact nor the pressure of a NATO, nor the emerging architecture of a regional Conference on Security and Cooperation in Europe (CSCE) as a guidepost. The model of Costa Rica—general and complete disarmament—was favored by a number of participants. What could be the rationale for any security system in the post cold war era if there were no threat? Superpower rivalries that had fed the regional conflict were gone, and so, by inference, was the need for anything beyond a Costa Rica style constabulary. Even Cuba, it appeared, could not hold out much longer as a revolutionary force.

His Excellency Eduardo Vallarino, Panamanian ambassador to the United States, had a differing perspective, as did several others. He noted in his address to the conference that, even between the time of Noriega's ouster and the date of the conference, his country had undergone a change of heart on this point. As an example, during the period of initial euphoria, plans for the purchase of twelve naval patrol boats were canceled. As the country moved back toward a more somber assessment, however, triggered in the particular instance of the patrol boats by acts of banditry on the seas, the purchase of the patrol boats was quickly reinstated. More broadly, the very definition of the nation-state incorporates the element of the monopoly of legitimate force. Skeptical conferees had trouble imagining any region of 25 million people wholly abandoning the concept of national armies or moving rapidly to an integrated transnational military force. Europe failed in its effort to create the European Defense Community, and it took the Soviet threat and American leadership to transform NATO from a treaty to an alliance.

The conference explored, but rejected, the idea of a new regional security system led by the United States. The United States, on the one hand, has in place arrangements to contend with Cuba and the Soviet submarine presence in the unlikely event of new cold war tensions. There is no need, from the standpoint of current U.S. security needs, for altering the consultative mechanisms already in place. Any new security system, on the other hand, should be designed to meet a genuine security threat. Because no one could come up with such a threat, despite the effort of several participants to propose drug trafficking as the rationale, there was no compelling case for a new U.S.-led security system in the region. Latin sensitivities to any expanded U.S. military role, as well as mistakes resulting from the disproportionate weight of defense concerns in past aid packages, further dim the appeal of a wider U.S. role in the region's internal security concerns. The help that the United States and other nations can provide on the issues of security and stability probably lies in the broader economic and technical assistance area and in pressure on the human rights issue to sustain the economic and political reform processes under way.

RECENT TRENDS AND A LOOK TO THE FUTURE

In the period since the conference, the peace process in Central America has appeared to inch forward along the path discernible at the time. The UN-sponsored peace talks in El Salvador have moved tortuously toward a successful resolution of the conflict. The talks received a dramatic boost with the March 1991 legislative elections in which moderate leftist parties made a good showing and the governing rightist ARENA party lost its absolute parliamentary majority. For the first time, the electoral process in El Salvador was open to all points of view, which the Left had insisted upon as a precondition for ending the war. The senior military commander of the Salvadoran rebel army, Joaquin Villalobos, asserted in a March 1991 speech in Mexico City that the FMLN could no longer be considered a "Marxist" movement and that the idea of one-party rule in El Salvador would be "absurd." His coalition's goals would not be achieved through armed revolution, but through participation as an unarmed political movement in a new pluralistic and competitive democracy.[2]

On the other side, San Salvador Mayor Armando Calderon Sol, a founding member of the ARENA party, said in a Washington interview at the end of March that "We understand that peace is indispensable for democracy and economic development" and that he was "optimistic that we will be successful" in the negotiations.[3] Neither the murder of an American helicopter crew by guerrillas nor the Salvadoran government's failure to investigate fully the 1989 assassination of six Jesuit priests has been enough to produce serious changes

2. Mark A. Uhlig, "Top Salvadoran Rebel Alters His Goals," *New York Times*, March 2, 1991, p. A3.
3. Al Kamen, "El Salvador's Factions Say Civil War May Be Nearing Resolution," *Washington Post*, April 7, 1991, p. A24.

in U.S. policy nor to derail the peace process. A cease-fire, ending the decade-long civil war that cost more than 70,000 lives, appeared to be in sight. The cease-fire would apparently begin with an agreement to separate the combatants, which would give the rebels temporary security zones where they could remain armed pending a final cease-fire and further accords toward demobilization. The next stage would involve massive reductions in the 60,000-man Salvadoran armed forces, full civilian control over the military, stripping the army of many police and public order functions, and investigating those responsible for human rights abuses.[4]

In Nicaragua, the admission that Sandinista army officers had shipped sophisticated weapons to Salvadoran rebels was ignored when Mrs. Chamorro absolved her Sandinista-dominated military command of responsibility. The murder of former contra leader Enrique Bermudez stirred fears of a revival of internal tensions. The Sandinistas condemned the act and disavowed responsibility. Mrs. Chamorro continued to walk a tightrope with her still-formidable Sandinista-controlled army and police apparatus. Yet, in one year she had succeeded in reducing the army from 80,000 to 28,000 enlisted men (and the officer corps from 15,000 to 10,000) and in cutting the military budget to one-third its former level. Land disputes in northern Nicaragua, however, plagued implementation of the agreement under which the contras laid down their arms following the Sandinista electoral defeat. Although some 7,700 former contras have received government farmland as part of the settlement ending the war, most of this land has been in southern and eastern Nicaragua, where government-owned land is plentiful. The bulk of the estimated 20,000 demobilized contras have returned to their homes in the northern mountains where land is scarce and the number of legal disputes over titles to land has been increasing. A band of approximately 200 disenchanted former contras, dubbed "re-contras" by the local peasants, have taken up arms again in the northern mountains, alleging that

4. On April 30, 1991, the Salvadoran National Assembly approved a pact reached the week before between the government and the FMLN. This pact stripped the Salvadoran military of some of its security functions and its virtually autonomous status and outlined constitutional reforms that would take effect on the successful conclusion of ongoing cease-fire negotiations. In the meantime the war continued, apparently in its final stages. The FMLN asserted that in April it had inflicted 691 casualties on government troops, taken 23 prisoners, and destroyed 132 electrical installations around the country. The government, however, reported the fighting at much lower levels.

the Sandinista-controlled army and police are failing to honor owner-ship rights of former contra fighters. These new contras have no out-side support and to date have engaged in no significant military activ-ity. But this could change, particularly if the Sandinista army disrupts the peace process in Salvador by providing arms and support to die-hards within the rebel coalition.

In Guatemala, the United States in December 1990 cut off a $3.3 million annual aid program to protest the army's refusal to investigate two ranking military officers implicated in the murder of an American innkeeper. The new president, Jorge Serrano Elias, revived and trans-ferred the judicial proceedings from remote Peten province to the capital soon after his election in January 1991. The State Department and U.S. drug enforcement officials welcomed the president's efforts in bringing the case to trial as a step toward resumed U.S. aid and toward wider U.S.-Guatemala collaboration in drug enforcement ac-tivities in the region.

In Panama, a quixotic coup attempt by former military officers was put down easily, and then ignored. The first attempted military coup in the region in six years, it seemed a parody of the image of military domination of a weak civilian society. At the same time, the massive U.S. assault that removed Noriega from power could not be said to have produced a stable and strong democracy after more than a year.

Press and other media coverage of events in Central America has slowed markedly; the number of correspondents is down to the levels that prevailed before the Sandinista revolution in 1979. Typical of this reversal of public and media attention in North America is the Janu-ary 1991 trip by former Nicaraguan President Daniel Ortega to Bagh-dad in an effort to inject himself as an intermediary into the Gulf cri-sis. Aside from a few wordless seconds on American television, he was totally ignored. The vastly reduced temperature of Central Amer-ican issues in Congress and in the media testifies to the effect of Pres-ident Bush's decision early in his administration to remove the re-gion's conflicts as a focus of partisan battles in the United States. Whether this was a wise decision that will help clear the way toward a solution of the regional crisis—or a signal of withdrawal that will leave unsolved the core problems—will depend on the U.S. commit-ment to such new initiatives as the Partnership for Democracy and Development and on the skill and resourcefulness of Central Ameri-ca's emerging democratic leadership.

MARK B. ROSENBERG

Strengthening
Democratic Institutions

The burst of anticipation that accompanied the return to democracy throughout Latin America in the 1980s has been sobered by the enduring economic difficulties there. Although Latin America's economic problems are far from solved, it is clear that the continuing commitment to democracy augurs well for the region.

Nowhere is this better illustrated than in Central America. From Guatemala to Panama, discussion and debate center on means and methods for expanding political participation and strengthening democratic institutions and the rule of law. The positive regional climate for democracy is complemented by dynamic change in the international system that will force Central America to accelerate its capacity for economic and political responsiveness.

This chapter focuses on the range of political issues that will inform Central America's prospects for maintaining and enhancing democracy during the 1990s. It presents general lessons that have been learned about democracy from the 1980s, questions what we know about democracy in Central America and its problems, and asks what can be done during this decade to enhance democracy and its prospects.

GENERAL LESSONS FROM THE 1980S

Three lessons from the 1980s inform this analysis. First, although democracy has many meanings, it is clear that Latin Americans themselves are less interested in the scholarly debates over the means and ends of democracy and more interested in simply establishing and maintaining the means to achieve democracy. In country after country, constitutionalists, party officials, and public affairs leaders have devoted unprecedented attention to the political arrangements and procedural features of constructing and consolidating democracy. Emphasis has been given to the formal and informal institutional arrangements that are necessary to create and sustain democracy.

Then, pitched rhetorical battles continue to be fought over whether the values and culture of the region actually promote or undermine democracy in the region. From the experience of the 1980s, however, it is clear that people in the region seem to want democracy and the open political environment and political freedom accompanying democratic rule.

Finally, following nearly two decades of soul-searching, there seems to be an understanding in the United States of the importance of democracy in Latin America and the fragility of the democratic political environment there. In the 1990s, there should be few competitive U.S. policy interests that contradict, undermine, or otherwise diminish U.S. efforts to support democracy throughout Latin America and the Caribbean.

THE RECENT EXPERIENCE WITH DEMOCRACY IN CENTRAL AMERICA

To understand the policy options that should be exercised in the 1990s in Central America to support democracy, one must first review the experience of the last decade in the region.

The Political Process

There seems to be a general appreciation of the fact that democracy in Central America, as elsewhere, has emerged as the second best option for most national groups. Less well-understood, however, is the notion that compromise and conciliation are a continuing part of the democratic process rather than a momentary feature of a transition from military to civilian rule. The difficulties in understanding the need for compromise are as intense within most political parties as across them.

A critical dimension of compromise is the development of "pacts" among key political actors. Such pacts serve as an outline for disagreement within predefined boundaries that are introduced to safeguard the constitutional groundwork upon which the democracy has been established in the first place. Of course, for several countries of the region, such pacts are problematic when there are armed minorities that reject civility as a legitimate end in itself.

Further, there is as yet little appreciation of the fact that democracy tends to enhance political uncertainty. The opening of political space or empowerment of previously repressed groups or newly formed groups may tend to frustrate them and the objects of their political energies, especially if there are only nascent mechanisms for channeling their concerns.

It is also clear that there is no necessary relationship between democracy and efficient government, social justice, or economic well-being.[1] In the short run, the return to democracy may actually accelerate corruption and inefficiency, social injustice, and economic inequities. Thus, although most Central American countries have passed the minimum necessary economic and sociocultural levels for stable democratic rule to emerge, there are no guarantees about who shall benefit how much or in what proportion to others in the emerging democratic environment of Central America.[2]

The civil-military dynamic is a critical issue in Central America's political process. Weak political institutions, uncertain political leadership, and the military's control of arms continue to contribute to the armed forces' high profile in Central American politics. The most disturbing feature of civil-military relations in the 1980s, however, is that civilians in and out of Central America have had little success in pushing the military back into the barracks. If this is ever to happen, it will have to be effected by more aggressive civilian efforts to pare the military's large domain and to increase its accountability to civilian officials.

1. Samuel Huntington, "The Modest Meaning of Democracy," in Robert Pastor, ed., *Democracy in the Americas: Stopping the Pendulum* (Holmes and Meier, 1989), p. 25.
2. As reported by Mitchell Seligson, "There appears to be a lower threshold of economic and sociocultural development beneath which stable democratic rule is unlikely to emerge. The income threshold appears to be around $250 per capita in 1957 dollars, and the sociocultural threshold, usually defined by educational achievement, seems to be the reduction of illiteracy to below 50 percent." James M. Malloy and Mitchell Seligson, eds., *Authoritarians and Democrats: Regime Transition in Latin America* (University of Pittsburgh Press, 1987), p. 7.

The Institutional Framework

For democracy to be effective, core democratic institutions must have both the legitimacy and capacity to address public needs. Following a decade of elections in Central America, there is now greater understanding that fair and honest elections are a necessary, but hardly sufficient, first step in developing and maintaining democracy.

Even in a context of post-Keynesian economics and austerity/shock politics, governments must have public sectors that function. Planning, intersectoral coordination, and competence are still major challenges. Inexperienced leadership coupled with unremitting demands for jobs and sinecures from party loyalists lead to institutional immobility. In such a context, corruption becomes a rational means to manage pressure. Privatization is a useful option to advance productivity and efficiency in some, but not all, sectors of the public sector. The rhetoric about privatization of the public sector, however, is inversely proportional to the capacity to effect it, especially in certain socially sensitive areas under state control (that is, electricity, water, and sewage). The resulting political mobilization against privatization among public employees has contaminated efforts made to privatize those publicly held assets that could benefit and flourish under private sector control.

Central America's tradition of weak legislatures is a problem endemic to Latin America legislatures. The legislative art is critical to the continuing work of a democracy, however, and can serve as the key public forum for channeling political energies. Indeed, artful cooperation between the executive and legislative branches may be a key to reducing the military presence in national politics throughout the region. There is probably a direct correlation between the legislature's credibility as an institution and its ability to effect positive changes in civil-military relations.

To varying degrees, executives have little trust for legislatures and prefer to use executive decrees whenever possible to forward their initiatives. Indeed, most legislatures in the region have limited institutional capacity for policy initiation, their professionalism is low, and their accountability skills over the executive are nascent.

One of the significant problems with legislatures in Central America is the lack of public understanding about their role in democratic governance. There are few nongovernment groups, however, that really understand the potential of their legislature for serving as a forum of discussion, debate, and review. This is particularly true with the region's private sector, which tends to be more adept at educating the U.S. Congress than its own national congresses.

Judiciaries are another critical element in the institutional equation of Central America, particularly if the military's influence and power are to be limited. Justice issues can be broadly conceptualized to involve a range of actors, including government agencies (police, prosecutors, courts, corrections) and nongovernmental groups (lawyers). During the past decade in Central America, certain groups have managed to remain outside the range of effective judicial accountability and others, through political manipulation, have maintained their traditional privileged status. The continuing civil war in several countries has reduced a weak justice system to impotence in politically related crimes.

Although justice systems face severe tests in responding to political and civil crimes, there are equally serious challenges in the fields of commercial and environmental law. In the former, changing relations of international production and technology are already placing extraordinary demands on local legal systems in Central America. Environmental issues are now priority items among international agency concerns as the dimension of environmental deterioration is finally being recognized.

The Art of Governance

The fluid nature of Central American politics and the congeries of political forces targeting the political arena give even greater imperative to the need for attention to the crafting of the political good life. "The difference between political survival or breakdown is a question of 'political crafting.'"[3] Undoubtedly, many lessons in political crafting have been learned throughout the 1980s in Central America. There seem to be several key elements to crafting that are not necessarily unique to the region. First, civilian empowerment is critical. The main objective has been, and should continue to be, the democratic control of military, police, and intelligence systems. Small steps

3. Juan Linz and Alfred Stepan, "Political Crafting of Democratic Consolidation or Destruction: European and South American Comparisons," in Pastor, ed., *Democracy in the Americas*, p. 41.

have been taken toward this end in Central America during the last decade. Considerable progress should be made in this decade if peace agreements can be articulated between governments and ideological extremists.

Second, as José Napoleón Duarte commented, "democracy cannot exist without a viable opposition and without an opposition there is no democracy."[4] Stated in other terms, "for democratic consolidation to occur, a variety of 'potential' democrats must be given the benefit of the doubt."[5] Throughout the 1980s, there was growing discipline and maturity among Central American governments and oppositions. A critical aspect of this evolution related to the conflict between those in power and the free press. Such tensions led to public dialogue between elected and press leaders in several Central American countries as a means to mitigate hostilities.

Ultimately, the responsibility for political crafting rests with the broad array of Central America's political leaders at both the national and local levels. There seems to be a growing recognition of this fact. The 1990s will be decisive if the political good life in Central America is to be achieved.

ENHANCING CENTRAL AMERICAN DEMOCRACY IN THE 1990S

The new spirit of cooperation between the United States and the Soviet Union has clear implications for Central America. For the first time since World War II, the possibility of a threat to U.S. national security emanating from a new Soviet proxy in the region is significantly diminished. As a result of these changes, the 'J.S. interest in Central America is assuming new forms and dimensions. As the United States focuses its attention on other world areas following a decade of unprecedented attention to Central America, there will be a reduction in U.S. economic assistance to the region.

Even as the external threat diminishes for Central American poli-

4. Max G. Manwaring, ed., "Uncomfortable Wars: Some Practitioners Speak," January 1990, p. 107.
5. Laurence Whitehead, "The Consolidation of Fragile Democracies: A Discussion with Illustrations," in Robert Pastor, ed., *Democracy in the Americas,* p. 77.

ties, serious internal problems remain. In difficult circumstances, democracy emerged throughout the region in the 1980s as a response to crisis. If democracy is to continue in the 1990s, however, measures must be taken to support fragile democratic institutions. What are these measures?

Supporting the Political Process

The key efforts to support the political process in Central America were initiated by President Oscar Arias of Costa Rica. The Esquipulas II Agreement and its subsequent variations empowered Central American leaders with the confidence and the instruments to negotiate a range of options for addressing political differences within the region and within their respective countries. The recent meeting of Central American heads of state to discuss new measures for economic integration is the latest, and, perhaps, most important, variant of Central American cooperative efforts. Although these discussions will inevitably open old wounds from previous integration efforts, they send an important message of the need for cooperation and consensus throughout the region and to would-be public and private partners throughout the globe.

For a new Central America to emerge in the 1990s, however, peace efforts must succeed in both El Salvador and Guatemala. Although there seems to be a general recognition that military solutions are counterproductive to the consolidation of democracy, political violence continues apace. It is in Central America's interest, however, to ensure that negotiations are successfully concluded in each of these countries and that contending factions are pacified. Without this pacification, it will be very difficult to develop the regional confidence necessary to respond to the growing social agenda in each of the countries.

Pacification of contending military forces, however, is a prelude to a more difficult issue that confronts a number of Central American countries. In Nicaragua and Panama the formal and informal "rules of the game" are still very much in dispute as contending political forces jockey for power in the new democratic environment. In Nicaragua a modus vivendi seems to have been established as a result of direct negotiations between contending forces. In Panama a governing coalition is now cautiously restructuring a highly mobilized political arena.

The fundamental issues that confront both Costa Rica and Honduras revolve around their respective economies. In the former, pressures are mounting for major government cutbacks. In the latter, a new austerity package threatens to undermine the current president's ability to govern.

Honduras and Costa Rica appear in the most privileged position in the region because their fundamental problems revolve around issues of economic management. Even if Guatemala and El Salvador can pacify and incorporate groups given to political violence and militarism, then "new rules of the game" will have to be established. Likewise, should Nicaragua and Panama effect consensus on the new formal and informal "rules of the game," then each will still confront significant economic problems.

The prospects for success in these challenges are, at best, uneven. During the 1990s, the critical threats to democracy will be largely internal. Corruption is a serious problem in most of the countries of the region, where healthy appetites for illicit gain were developed in the last two decades as a result of unprecedented external private and public funding. As the U.S. experience illustrates, however, democracy is not an antidote to illicit gain. The issue becomes even more complicated as the transnational possibilities for illegal activity multiply as drug-traffickers and others target the region as an important communication point in transit to the United States.

Another threat emanates from the military, which remains one of the strongest institutions in the region. With the exception of Costa Rica, military establishments still play an important political role in each of the countries of the region. Although there seems to be consensus that the military's role in politics must be reduced if democracy is to be maintained, there are few instances in Central America where civilians have had the political will or technical capacity to effect the necessary changes.

Moreover, a potentially serious threat to democracy looms on the horizon as the United States pursues an aggressive antinarcotics strategy in Latin America. An unanticipated consequence of this strategy may be to "encourage the violation of weak constitutional norms" in the pursuit of presumed drug-traffickers.[6] A concomitant problem relates directly to the military. U.S. efforts to militarize antinarcotics ef-

6. See "Prepared Statement of Eduardo Gamarra, Florida International University, before the Subcommittee on Western Hemisphere Affairs of the U.S. House of Representatives, Washington, D.C., June 6, 1990," p. 7.

forts in Central America may strengthen Central America's militaries at the very moment when they can be reduced in size, scope, and role. Indeed, U.S. support for the development of democratic institutions in Latin America is contradicted by U.S. support for extralegal methods of drug-enforcement. Policy planners and analysts must give special attention to the implications for Central American democracy of militarizing the antinarcotics efforts.

Enhancing the Institutional Framework for Democracy

Support for Central America's democratic institutions must be maintained and enhanced. At the most general level, the formal government institutions charged with maintaining democracy must be strengthened and empowered. Critical targets of support are judiciaries, legislatures, and electoral agencies. Several objectives that must be met include strengthening their capacity for autonomous initiative and independence, improving their technical capacity, and improving public and private sector awareness about the role and purpose of these institutions.

In almost every case in Central America, these critical institutions have only rudimentary capacity, incipient professionalism, and inefficient operations. Because they are on the front line of government efforts to maintain and expand legitimacy, they are more than incidental to the democratic process.

A major element to the enhancement of democratic institutions in Central America in the 1990s will be a reduction in the sphere of the military's domain.[7] Key areas that could be transferred to civilian control include law enforcement, customs, migration, merchant marine, airports, and seaports. If this transfer is to take place, political will and consensus among key civilian actors will be required.

A major problem in this regard, however, is the mobilization of expertise to assist Central American leaders in identifying priorities and strengthening targeted areas. For instance, there are only a handful of U.S. specialists who understand the strengths and weaknesses of the Central American legal system. There is only one agency in Cen-

7. See Alfred Stepan, *Rethinking Military Politics* (Princeton University Press, 1989), and Louis W. Goodman, Johanna S. R. Mendelson, and Juan Rial, *The Military and Democracy: The Future of Civil-Military Relations in Latin America* (Lexington, Mass.: Heath, 1990).

tral America that has expertise in providing technical assistance to strengthen electoral agencies. Beyond Costa Rica, there is little expertise in Central America in developing and enhancing legislative skill and capacity.

Simply strengthening key government institutions, however, is only part of the equation. Another critical element is the enhancement of awareness about the role that these institutions can play in providing access and accountability in the democratic process. At the government level, there has been little effort to understand and promote interagency coordination as a vehicle to expand responsiveness.

Indeed, for democracy to prosper during the 1990s, nongovernmental institutions will have to exercise greater coherence and vigor in overseeing and monitoring government activities. In some Central American countries, the Church has played a key role in this regard during the 1980s. In other countries, nonpartisan but politically oriented civic groups and an aggressive and/or responsive media have taken lead roles.

Beyond the formal institutional arena, key organizations will have to become more aggressive democratic players. Political parties, educational institutions, think tanks, labor unions, cooperatives, and private-sector organizations will need to learn about and understand their role in the democratic process. Although this is already taking place in some countries in the region, there is still a striking absence of local and community education about the possibilities and limits of democracy in the region.

Promoting the Art of Governing

One of the encouraging developments in Central America during the past decade has been the high-level involvement of senior statesmen from the United States and elsewhere in the quest for democracy, which provides confidence to leaders and would-be leaders about the art of governing. It is a crucial nontangible element of civilian empowerment that parallels the recurring interchanges and meetings of regional military leaders.

Efforts to bring Central American leaders together more frequently to discuss options for strengthening their democratic systems should be enhanced. These efforts should be led by leaders and former leaders from other democratic countries in Latin America with the concrete objective of identifying alternative approaches to enhancing the democratic political process and the institutional framework of democracy.

Ultimately, only the efforts of the Central Americans themselves can determine whether democracy will survive in Central America during the 1990s. Prospects for democracy in the region are better than at most other times in contemporary Central American history. For many in the region, however, democracy is still perceived as an inconvenient and burdensome experiment rather than as a permanent mode of political organization. The momentous task that lies ahead is to convince these individuals that democracy is a form that will guarantee even them a continuing role in the political process.

JULIO SERGIO RAMÍREZ

The Challenges for Democratization and Stability in the Emerging Poliarchies

This chapter presents some thoughts on several of the existing obstacles to consolidating the emerging democratic regimes in five of the six Spanish-speaking countries of the Central American isthmus.[1] It then suggests some possible courses of action for improving the stability and quality of the process of democratization in the region.

This is an exploratory effort—not a scholarly article or a formal proposal for policymaking—intended to stimulate debate on the subject of strengthening fragile democratic institutions.

The first section mentions several recent political events that help to illustrate the magnitude and potential impact of the current trends, as well as a few of the characteristics of the underlying structures that help to explain some of the major difficulties in consolidating democratic rule in the region. The second section deals with several concepts that are particularly useful in determining requirements and options for strengthening democracy in the region. The third section offers some suggestions for action, which at this stage are necessarily general, but that can be a useful starting point for further discussion of the urgent problem of consolidating the emerging democratic regimes in a region where that type of regime has been the exception rather than the rule.

THE STAGE

One can begin by pointing to some relevant facts and gratifying recent trends in the region. Since April 25, 1990, for the first time in their collective history, the six Spanish-speaking countries of the Cen-

---

1. I refer to Guatemala, El Salvador, Honduras, Nicaragua, and Panama as the emerging or transitional democracies of the region. I will exclude Costa Rica from the list, unless otherwise noted, because it is a stable and working democracy; nor will I include Belize.

tral American isthmus have civilian governments that came to power as a result of relatively open, free, competitive, and just elections (Panama is a special case). This is an important accomplishment because only a few years ago all the countries of the region, with the well-known exception of Costa Rica, were under military regimes.

—In the case of Nicaragua, for the first time since the formation of the Republic, more than 150 years ago, the opposition has been able to gain power, and the incumbent government has been willing to step down, after an intensively contested and fair election, without use of force.

—In the case of El Salvador, the last transfer of power in 1989 was the first between government and opposition as the result of an election since 1931.

—In Guatemala, the current government was the first to gain power through free and fair elections during the last three decades, and the coming elections in November would be the first, under a relatively free and competitive regime, after several decades of unscheduled or uncompetitive transfers of power.

—In Honduras, the last elections were the first competitive and open elections in which the opposition came to power peacefully during the last thirty years.

—In Costa Rica, another peaceful and competitive election transferred power to the opposition party in May.

There are, unfortunately, some negative points to be considered as well.

—The armies, in the five countries that have an army (Costa Rica, the exception again), are still in the barracks, but their transformation from political organizations to professional apolitical institutions is still in the initial stages; the temptation is strong to return to their former role as rulers of their countries.

—The majority of the main political parties in the five emerging poliarchies are not mass-based organizations with strong and stable electoral support; they have had very limited government experience; they have been established recently; and they have limited capabilities for interest articulation, interest representation, and leadership formation. Caudillism, personalism, and factionalism tend to weaken their effectiveness as political parties, and create enormous difficulties in strengthening the incipient democratic institutions.

—The most important pressure groups, as well as other intermediary institutions, have successfully obtained influence during the previous nondemocratic regimes by gaining favorable access to public officials through private and restricted channels, and not by means of developing capacities to formulate and represent their positions and interests in a more open and competitive public policy environment.

—The level of political violence, human rights abuses, and terrorism (from several different sides) is still important in at least three of the countries. The intensity of political and social hatred is very strong in Nicaragua and El Salvador, which are the two countries that have suffered civil war during the last decade. In El Salvador the war continues, and in Nicaragua peace has not yet been consolidated.

—The civilian governments in the five emerging poliarchies of the region are facing enormous challenges as a result of the combined impact of modernization, democratization, and economic mismanagement by their predecessors in office. Modernization breeds both economic and political instability owing to the heightened expectations and demands among various social groups. The initial stages of democratization are also highly unstable owing to the incipient development of the democratic institutions. The history of mankind illustrates the difficulty with which a large, complex, heterogeneous society develops a stable, open, and competitive political order. The level of economic deterioration throughout the region, excepting Costa Rica, is well known, and can be attributed principally to the policies and practices of the military or the ostensibly civilian, albeit military-controlled, regimes of recent years.

In summary, this group of countries is initiating a process of democratization despite enormous difficulties created by their weak democratic institutions and values, the uncertain loyalty to democratic principles among the key social actors, the legacy of violence and injustice in their recent history, and the expectations and demands of their modernizing—and hopefully resurrecting—civil societies.

USEFUL CONCEPTS ABOUT REAL-WORLD DEMOCRACIES OR POLIARCHIES

As presented by Robert Dahl in his illuminating work on the basic dimensions of democracy, political regimes in the real world are unlikely to fulfill the democratic ideal in terms of a government of the people, by the people, and for the people.[2] The reason is that in com-

2. Robert A. Dahl, *Poliarchy* (Yale University Press, 1971).

plex and modern societies, there are many obstacles owing to size, heterogeneity, inequality in the distribution of politically valuable resources, differences of opinion about what constitutes a good society, and social conflict among different sectors.

If perfect democracy is unlikely to exist, the practical problem is not how to build a fully democratic regime, but how to advance the degree of democratization of the existing one. Real-world democracies are then called poli-archies, in the sense of "the government of many" and as many as possible, as opposed to olig-archies, or "the government of the few," and, as contrasted with democracy, as "the government of all." "All" cannot govern, even indirectly through their representatives, as can be seen in reality. As the number of the "many" increases, the level of democratization rises, and the poliarchical regime comes closer to being a fully democratic one. Ultimately, a perfect poliarchy would be a democracy, since the "many" would become "all."

The degree of democratization of a political order can be determined by public contestation (public debate, or liberalization, or the ability to oppose or contest the government) and political participation. As a political regime increases the level of public contestation or of political participation, or both, its level of democratization increases. A highly liberalized and highly participatory regime would be a poliarchy. A completely liberalized and fully participatory regime would be a Democracy (with a capital "D").[3]

The recent political changes in the five Central American emerging (or potential) democracies have increased the levels of liberalization and political participation of their polities, and represent important advances in the long journey toward constructing stable democracies. Because these changes are only the beginning of a lengthy, and usually unstable, process, an examination of some of the key elements of democratization might be useful to suggest priorities for future actions.

Some Key Guarantees in a Democratic Political Order

There are greatly differing characteristics among contemporary democratic regimes. The following institutional guarantees sug-

3. Hereafter, to follow the common use of the term, the word democracy will be used in the sense of poliarchy as defined before. A reference to the perfect democracy will appear as Democracy (with a capital "D").

gested by Dahl could be considered essential for a political regime to be considered democratic:[4]

—Freedom to form and join organizations
—Freedom of expression
—The right to vote
—Eligibility for public office
—The right of political leaders to compete for support
—Alternative sources of information
—Free and fair elections
—Institutions requiring government policies that are dependent upon votes and other expressions of preference.

This list can be separated into two parts—those guarantees that tend to be the result of the government's decision not to interfere with the rights of the political and social actors, and those that require significant and sustained effort by the government and other actors. The first group (the first six guarantees on the list) does not require significant and sustained effort by the government. The establishment of those guarantees depends on macropolicies, and can be accomplished in the short term; those are the guarantees needed to sustain the process of liberalization of the political system. The last two guarantees, and especially the last one, require the development of extensive institutional capabilities in the political system. These guarantees, which can be referred to as micropolicies, are usually lacking in incipient democracies because of the transition from authoritarian rule, and they are needed to sustain the process of participation in the political system.

In transitional and incipient democracies, it is easier to liberalize the polity than to give effective access and meaningful political participation to the citizenry. The first task depends mostly on government-controlled and available resources; the second task depends on institutional capabilities that need, among other requirements, time, significant amounts of resources from the government and from other social sectors, and ample and sustained support from the government and the key social and political actors.

Among the five emerging democracies of the region, major and significant institutional developments are needed to advance the process of democratization beyond the initial (and necessary) steps of liberal-

4. Dahl, *Poliarchy,* p. 3.

ization and electoral participation. The last section of this paper examines some of the critical needs.

The Purpose (or Justification) of a Democratic Regime

Why is the democratic form of government being promoted as the best form of government? At times one becomes so strongly identified with an idea that one tends to lose sight of the rationale.

It is arguable that, among the alternative forms of political order, the best is the one that affords society the greatest opportunity to choose a government that, in its decisionmaking process, will be most responsive to the needs and preferences of its citizens, all of whom are considered political equals.

From empirical observation among the existing regimes, it is clear that, in the complex, heterogeneous, and diverse societies of today, a democratic regime (one guaranteeing the aforementioned rights) tends to produce this type of government more consistently and frequently than the other existing alternatives.

Among the list of guarantees, the last one is the most difficult to achieve and maintain; frequently, it is not considered an essential feature of a democratic order, but simply as part of the development of a modern and efficient public sector. It must be emphasized that the last guarantee cannot be disregarded if the final justification for democratic rule is that it tends to produce governments that, in their decisionmaking process, are responsive to the needs and preferences of its citizens, all of whom are considered political equals. Without the last guarantee, the other guarantees will produce a liberalized and tolerant, but hardly democratic, government.

The Limitations of (or Obstacles to) a Democratic Rule

As indicated previously, the democratic process usually tends to produce governments that are sensitive to the needs and preferences of their citizens, but there are at least four major limitations that tend to inhibit democratic procedures, and these limitations are relevant in the current circumstances of the Central American countries.

1. When there is blatant inequality in the distribution and control of the economic, political, and social resources among the popula-

tion, a democratically elected government will tend to be more sensitive to the needs and preferences of those sectors that control the most important resources, because those sectors and their leaders will be the ones better able to influence government decisions. In this case, the relative weight that the government will give to the various sectors will be heavily influenced by the importance of the resources that those sectors command.

2. When there are large public bureaucracies that tend to operate independently of the elected officers, and have been effectively isolated from public scrutiny, the ability to influence government decisionmaking will frequently be limited to the election of the chief executive and the legislature. Indeed, this is hardly a satisfactory level of political participation, and tends to produce much frustration, dependency, and cynicism among the population.

3. When the basic consensus is weak or nonexistent, because of deep political or social conflicts, or both between important social sectors, it might be impossible to determine which needs and preferences the government should respond to and which it should ignore. Moreover, if the differences between major social sectors are too great, a democratic form of government will be highly unstable, and the political process might be extremely violent if it remains open and free. The cases of Nicaragua and El Salvador are examples of this limitation.

4. When one is dealing with small, poor, and highly indebted and dependent countries, the government decision process will be greatly influenced by the preferences and priorities of major and powerful external actors (either governments or agencies). In numerous instances, those preferences and priorities will undoubtedly conflict with those of large segments of the population.

The Impact of Modernization

The construction of stable democratic regimes has been one of the major recent achievements of human society. As recently as one hundred years ago, none of the existing political regimes in the world would qualify as democratic under today's standards—the most participatory and liberalized regimes of the last century excluded from electoral participation at least 50 percent of the adult population (women), restricted participation by additional requirements (property and literacy requisites), and excluded, either legally or effectively, racial minorities.

The impact of modernization on the then "restricted" poliarchies of Western Europe and North America at the beginning of this century was favorable in terms of creating pressures for the effective expansion of political rights to social groups that had been previously excluded from political participation. The process of expanding political rights was not a peaceful and ordered one, but a tumultuous and often violent struggle, which, in some important cases, ended only two decades ago (the southern black population of the United States).

The experiences of liberalization and democratization of previously hegemonic regimes in South America also tend to confirm the modernization paradox: modernization can be a strong factor for democratization because of the increasing capabilities among the social sectors for obtaining participation and liberalization. At the same time, modernization can be a catalyst for the advent of autocracy and dictatorship because of the potential for social disorder and violence among the previously excluded groups in their struggle to obtain access and rights.

Modernization increases the potential for creating a more democratic order, while simultaneously increasing the risks of ending that incipient regime or blocking its advent.

Conflict Regulation in Divided Societies

As previously indicated, a major obstacle to the democratic process in producing governments that are highly responsive to the needs and preferences of the citizens is the existence of deep conflicts between major social segments or groups. In those instances, the basic consensus is either nonexistent or very fragile, and the operation of the normal democratic process tends to be unstable and violent; therefore, a "competitive" democratic rule is unlikely to succeed.

An alternative form of government in which political competition is intentionally restricted by the leaders of the major feuding parties and segments, in an attempt to establish a viable and partially competitive political order, has been called "consociational" democracy. The experience of intensively divided societies that are ruled under successful consociational democracies helps to suggest some of the key provisions and practical arrangements that might be useful in facing the obstacle of intense divisions and in promoting a peaceful and stable democratic order in deeply divided societies.[5]

Among the conclusions that can be derived from the consociational cases, the following might be useful for the purpose of strengthening the democratic institutions of Central America:

—Majority rule must be replaced by a more consensus-based mechanism, especially in the divisive issues.

—The vital interests of all the major segments in conflict must be either formally or informally guaranteed.

—Political competition must be limited, both in terms of content (issues to be addressed) and impact (formal authority to be obtained through the electoral process).

—Consociational practices tend to restrict political competition, and should not be expected to last forever, if the purpose is to democratize the political system.

—Consociational arrangements are unstable, especially at the beginning of the new rule. Depending upon future developments, they can achieve stability or they can collapse under an increasing conflict.

—It is not always easy to differentiate a consociational arrangement that is developed by conflicting parties as the only alternative to violence and repression from an "oligopolistic" arrangement between major political groups that is intended to exclude other political actors from government by installing institutional provisions that favor the partners of the oligopoly.

In summary, the process of transition from authoritarian rule in five of the six Central American countries is progressing. The initial steps of liberalization are apparently advancing, but there are still enormous challenges to the consolidation of democratic rule in the region.[6] They must all effectively expand political participation, which gives meaningful roles in the polity to large segments of the population. They must reduce the negative influence of egregious inequality in the distribution of politically useful resources. They must subject large public bureaucracies to effective citizen control. They must

5. Eric A. Nordlinger, *Conflict Regulation in Divided Societies* (Harvard University, Center for International Affairs, 1972).

6. This tends to be the route of other recent transitions in Southern Europe and South America. See Guillermo O'Donnell, Phillippe Schmitter, and Lawrence Whitehead, eds., *Transitions from Authoritarian Rule* (Johns Hopkins University Press, 1966).

peacefully manage the intense political conflict in the two countries ravaged by civil war, and develop the necessary consociational practices that will support a stable process of democratization. They must improve the ability of the governments in the region to defend the interests of their citizens in their dealings with important and powerful external actors, and they must be able to manage successfully the impact of modernization, especially in terms of rising expectations and demands among large segments of the population.

KEY TASKS

The possibilities for strengthening a fragile or incipient democratic order depend on the sustained increase of the level of democratic institutionalization of those organizations, groups, values, roles, and procedures that will support that regime. The following are some of the most important groups and organizations and some of the tasks that could be performed for each of them to enhance their contribution toward consolidating a democratic order.

Initially, it is necessary to develop political parties, which are critical in the formation, strengthening, and functioning of a democratic regime.

—Organizational development: recruitment of membership, internal organization; specialization of roles (functional differentiation).

—Democratization of ideology, external practices, and internal structure and processes: level of allegiance of leaders and members to democratic rules; formal and effective support for democratic process even after electoral defeat; internal governance; membership participation; grass-roots development and participation.

—Leadership selection, formation, and control by the membership.

—Development of analytic skills in public policy: improving the understanding of complex public policy issues among the party leaders; formulation of consistent policies and priorities.

—Negotiation and strategy formulation skills, coalition formation, dialogue, consensus building.

They must then develop other key intermediary institutions, whose role is to mediate between society and state. Under hegemonic regimes, such institutions tend to have little or no influence and to be underdeveloped, fragile, and dependent. Among the intermediary organizations could be selectively included: Pressure groups—both private and public; voluntary and nonprofit organizations; communal and regional organizations; and cultural, educational, artistic, and ethnic organizations.

The areas of development could include organizational development; skills for strategy formulation and implementation; democratization of structure and internal processes; leadership selection, formation, and control; analytic skills in public policy issues in the fields of their interest and legitimacy; negotiation and interest representation skills.

The next improvement should focus upon the institutions of control, which are among the most important and sensitive in a democratic order. These institutions have been a major source of oppression against society and have caused widespread frustration and anger in the previous military regime.

—Judicial and penal systems, that constitute the active, formal, and real means for legal domination of society by the state, as practiced extensively and brutally in hegemonic regimes. They are also the active, formal, and real means for legal protection of the rights of the individual against the abusive use of power by the state or by other parties, as practiced extensively in democratic regimes.

—Institutions in charge of maintaining the responsiveness and accountability of public officials, because the issues of corruption, nepotism, domination, and existence of very restrictive channels for influencing government decisions are among the most serious obstacles to creating a civic order.

—Coercive forces such as the police and the military should be democratized. Because they are the necessary physical instrument of a regime, whether democratic or not, they can work to achieve either state domination of society, or the submission of the citizens and their leaders (the military and the police included) to the rule of law.

This process of democratization of the coercive forces could start with the formation of groups of civic soldiers or policemen through an educational process that is oriented to creating civic attitudes and strengthening the democratic values and behavior among the military and police personnel. To increase the potential for developing a coercive apparatus whose behavior is more civilized and supportive of a democratic rule, and ever mindful of the severe budgetary restrictions of all the countries involved, this process might require a significant reduction in the size and the budget of the military and police establishment.

The process of peaceful and ordered public debate and communication must also be strengthened. This refers not only to the press, but also to the other means of communication, dialogue, and consensus formation in society, especially between the key political and social actors. This effort will be particularly important in El Salvador and Nicaragua—the two countries that have suffered civil war during the last decade and that are still deeply divided.

Finally, they must expand citizen access to, and representation in, the political system; improve the electoral system to increase its fairness and reliability; and develop additional and extensive means and channels for influencing public policy by the citizenship. The development of the political parties and the other abovementioned intermediary institutions will help to support and utilize this expansion.

Strategies for
Economic Development

Central America today is in a unique position to press forward on the development front. At no time in the region's history have so many governments and organizations been interested in helping the region to stabilize and grow. At no time has there been so much money available to finance development. At no time has there been the urgency to recover, rebuild, and integrate to form a viable economic region and market that can participate in regional and world trade.

It is clear today that there are no choices for Central America. The countries of the region *must* mature both politically and economically or be left hopelessly behind other countries in this hemisphere and elsewhere in the developing world.

THE PRESENT SITUATION

To understand what Central America must accomplish in the coming years, it is useful to understand its current relative position. A few numbers will help to establish the baseline.

Between 1981 and 1989 all Latin America registered its worst decade of growth in the postwar period, with an increase of regional domestic product of only 11.7 percent (CEPAL) as compared with a doubling of gross domestic produce (GDP) between 1970 and 1980 (IDB).[1] Performance in the Central American economies during the decade of the 1980s was mixed. Costa Rica grew by 20.9 percent and Honduras by 19.8. Panama grew only 0.4 percent, mostly because of a 16.4 percent drop in 1988. El Salvador's economy shrank by 6.3 percent and Nicaragua's by 9.6.

1. CEPAL stands for Comision Economica para America Latina y el Caribe (Economic Commission for Latin America and the Caribbean). IDB is the Inter-American Development Bank.

For Latin America as a whole, per capita growth was down by 8 percent from 1982 to 1989 (CEPAL). Even with large-scale out-migration, Central America's population grew at nearly 3 percent a year in the 1980s. As a consequence, per capita GDPs declined: by 6 percent in Costa Rica, 12 percent in Honduras, 17–18 percent in El Salvador, Guatemala, and Panama, and 33 percent in Nicaragua (CE-PAL). Per capita incomes in every country were substantially less in 1988 than in 1980; in El Salvador and Nicaragua they were less than in 1970. Today it is estimated that two-thirds of the population in Central America lives in conditions of poverty; almost 40 percent live in extreme poverty and 23.3 percent cannot satisfy basic needs. Except for Costa Rica, more than half the population in each country lives in extreme poverty.

Population continues to grow. The region's population doubled to 25 million people in the twenty-five years between 1960 and 1985, and it is estimated that it will reach 33 million by 1995. The population under sixteen years of age represents 45.6 percent of the total population in the region; it approaches 50 percent in Nicaragua, Honduras, El Salvador, and Guatemala. Against this tragic background, it is estimated that over 14 percent of the population of the five countries has migrated out of country or is internally displaced. Urban unemployment has tripled in the decade.

Gross domestic investment fell from approximately 24 percent of regional GDP to 16 percent in all of Latin America during the 1980s. Investment declined even more sharply in Central America. In Costa Rica it fell from almost 30 percent of GDP in 1980 to 23.4 percent in 1987. Investment was already low in El Salvador in 1980 and stood at 12.9 percent of GDP in 1987. In Guatemala it was 11.5 percent of GDP in 1987 and in Honduras it fell from 26 percent of GDP in 1980 to 13.8 percent in 1987. Foreign investment follows domestic investment, and, by the end of the 1980s, foreign investors had nearly abandoned Central America. Foreign direct investment ranged from 5.3 percent of investment in El Salvador to 9.5 percent in Honduras, 15.4 percent in Costa Rica, and 28.5 percent in Guatemala, the largest economy.

Although every country but El Salvador and Nicaragua has increased its exports over the past decade, the mix of exports has tended to concentrate on traditional agricultural products, and the purchasing power of export goods has fallen 61 percent in El Salvador, 46 percent in Nicaragua, and 26 percent in Guatemala. Rates declined 2.6 percent in Honduras and increased by 24.7 percent in Costa Rica—the only country that has succeeded in substantially increasing its nontraditional exports.

Numbers like these are clearly unacceptable. They describe a crisis of major proportions that will require concerted attention for many years to come. Even the five-year planning horizons recommended by the Kissinger and Sanford commissions are too short to ensure visible successes.

THE CHOICES FOR DEVELOPMENT

The Central American crisis has been studied by many institutions, individuals, and commissions. Their recommendations will fill a library shelf. The United Nations Program for Cooperation in Central America (PEC) has compiled an abbreviated list of more than ninety-eight project sectors that have been recommended for attention in the region.

Fortunately, both government multilateral institutions and bilateral donors have begun to implement the recommendations of these many commissions. Equally fortunately, although they may emphasize one or another particular aspect of Central American recovery, the commissions are consistent in concluding that in the aftermath of a decade of economic crisis and adjustment, there are very few alternatives available to Central America. Energetic reform with an eye to growth, income and employment generation, and insertion into the global economy is the sine qua non of recovery. The question that policymakers must answer is how to best and most efficiently implement that reform—maximizing the economic effect while minimizing the negative impacts on social equity.

In this regard, Central America is not unlike every other world region that is seeking to integrate itself into the world economy. We can reflect on IMF Managing Director Michel Camdessus's recommendations to the nations of Eastern Europe:

From our experience so far with the reforming countries, and with the rest of the membership, I would draw a few lessons.

—First, the attempts to find a "third way" intermediate between central planning and a market economy have not been successful;

—Second, . . . it is probably a mistake to adopt a piecemeal approach, because all the elements of the economic system are related;

—Third, economic reforms will only work well if they take place in an environment of strong financial discipline;

—Fourth, we really do not know how long it will take for the reforms to produce a supply response;

Finally, governments that are introducing systemic reforms can increase their chances of success if they aim at:

—Firm macroeconomic policies that establish a framework of financial stability and are conducive to steady, medium-term growth;

—Structural reforms that establish an appropriately decentralized system of decision making and responsibility, and an effective pattern of incentives—to work, to save and to invest;

—A regulatory framework to supervise and maintain the market infrastructure and to decide delicate and complex distributional issues; and, finally, and most essential for the transitional period;

—A social safety net . . . to cushion the impact of unemployment by supporting and retraining the unemployed and to alleviate the human cost of adjustment for the most vulnerable parts of the population.

In addition, Camdessus noted that "the reforming countries cannot succeed on their own. They will require considerable help from abroad and a readiness on the part of the advanced industrial countries, in particular, to expand their trading links."[2]

The present time is particularly propitious for examining the Central American situation and for renewing the commitment to positive outcomes. There has been a diminution of the conflicts that previously made planning for the midterm difficult, attracting investment almost impossible, and that have multiplied the social and reconstruction burdens on the states in the region. Hopefully they will shortly cease altogether. There are no winners in the cycle of violence.

It is particularly heartening to see the Latin American consensus endorsing the reform process recommended by Camdessus. Latin American leaders have learned the hard way that they must either

2. From Michel Camdessus's speech, "The IMF's Role in Promoting Economic Reform in Eastern Europe and Other Planned Economies," delivered before the Royal Institute of International Affairs and Overseas Development Institute in London, April 19, 1990.

become competitive in the world market or fall hopelessly and permanently behind.

Becoming competitive is not an easy task, however. John Williamson's study of the progress of policy reform in Latin America over the past decade suggests strongly that although one is surely damned if one does not undertake reform, one cannot be assured of success if one does attempt reform.[3] More important for political leaders, one cannot be sure of the timing of success.

Williamson identified ten areas of reform that constitute the current agenda for adjustment. Some duplicate the IMF managing director's agenda; others go beyond it: fiscal discipline; public spending cuts; tax reform; financial (interest rate) liberalization; exchange rate competitiveness; trade liberalization; foreign direct investment; privatization; deregulation; and property rights.

Central America must act on each of these fronts. And, beyond these agenda items, Central American countries must also face the challenge of stabilizing displaced populations, basic education, training of more than 50 percent of most populations for participation in complex agriculture, commercial or industrial activities, and essential institution building. These achievements must take place at the same time as basic infrastructure is reconstructed and rehabilitated and economies and societies are reoriented.

It will not suffice merely to restore the economic quality of life of precrisis Central America. Rather, we envision an entirely new and different Central America—open to the outside world; trading products other than coffee, sugar, and cotton; in which the majority of the people are not illiterate nor lacking in basic health services; in which unemployment touches a few, not the many; and in which Central Americans themselves have confidence and invest. How to achieve that new state of affairs is the question.

THE CHALLENGE OF ECONOMIC ADJUSTMENT

In looking at the process of economic adjustment in Central America, everything is related. As Michel Camdessus noted, it is probably a mistake to adopt a piecemeal approach. Each of the policy areas iden-

3. Latin American Adjustment: How Much Has Happened? (Washington: Institute for International Economics, 1990).

tified by Williamson must be tackled directly, but the time frames for implementation and playout are variable and sometimes lengthy. The social insecurity remaining from the 1980s crisis and internal turmoil may compromise the prospects of success of policy reform. Social stabilization must be undertaken on an urgent basis.

During the June 1990 weekend summit of Central American leaders, the five regional presidents resolved to work toward restructuring and strengthening Central American integration and the Central American Common Market (CACM), which has been a casualty of the crisis of the 1980s. Regional integration is an important goal and can stimulate both export production and new investments by providing attractive economies of scale and complementary relationships. It is important to remember, however, that the new integrated market will have to be substantially different from the old one, and it may have to promote activities considerably different from those that benefited from the old CACM.

The CACM evolved under an import-substituting industrialization strategy. Extraregional trade remained essentially agricultural in orientation during the market's heyday. Intraregional trade in industrial products increased during the 1970s, but declined sharply after the 1980s crisis began. Traditional commodity exports, which highly protected consumer manufacturers grew in the protected intraregional market, continued to be the important earners of hard currencies.

It is now generally acknowledged that an ISI development strategy is no longer appropriate in today's interdependent and competitive world economic environment. Exports will be the engine of Central American growth in the coming decade and beyond. Central American integration will provide a regional production base that can undertake economies of scale. But Central America's most important task in the coming years will be to expand nontraditional exports to extraregional markets that will pay in hard currencies, while building a regional market that is attractive to investors; that is sufficiently diversified to permit countries to weather fluctuation in individual sector performance, and that generates employment for the very large segment of each country's population that exists below the poverty line.

Costa Rica has been the only regional country to apply successfully this export diversification scheme in the 1980s, and it has succeeded largely on the basis of expansion of agricultural and horticultural products, not manufactures. An economic renewal based on liberalization of trade to extraregional markets may well bypass many of the consumer products industries that developed under the protected regime of the 1960s and 1970s and that have been starved for incomes during the 1980s. Central American leaders will have to resist the temptation to ease the lot of inefficient and noncompetitive manufacturers. Future aid donors will have to identify the most competitive new products and orient the reconstruction of infrastructure—ports, airports, warehouses, feeder roads, and customs procedures that will support the new export orientation.

Another feature of the industrialization promoted under the Common Market was that it tended to be capital, not labor, intensive. With population growth rates greater than 3 percent and nearly 50 percent of the population entering the labor market over the next decade and beyond, Central America cannot afford capital-intensive growth.[4] Every consideration must be given to the employment generation prospects of investment decisions.

Another policy area that Central American governments will have to tackle and that, if recent experience offers any lesson, will surely generate political resistance, is tax reform. Export taxes have been a favorite form of revenue generation for Latin American governments. In Central America, except Nicaragua, over 25 percent of current government revenues have been generated by taxes on international trade. The World Bank calculates that the average ratio of export taxes to revenue for lower middle-income countries is only 15 percent. To stimulate exports, government will have to shift from export taxes to other revenue-generating means—especially to income taxes—and to insist on greater compliance by taxpayers.

In this area, Central Americans can take heart at the experience of countries as diverse as Bolivia and Mexico that have undertaken to reform tax collection. Mexican Finance Minister Pedro Aspe recently told an international audience that Mexico had determined that to get its prices right and to attract investment Mexico had to have a tax structure that was internationally competitive. Revenues would be

---

4. For a discussion of the resources required to ensure job creation in Latin America, see Margaret Daly Hayes, "U.S. Security, Economic Growth and the Population Problem in Latin America," in John Saunders, ed., *Population Growth in Latin America and U.S. National Security* (Winchester, Mass.: Allen and Unwin, 1986), and the World Bank's *World Development Report, 1984.*

generated by lowering tax rates and broadening the tax base. Early reports of Mexico's progress in this area are very good.

Increased investment means greater commitment by the region's private sector. Domestic entrepreneurs will have to demonstrate their faith in their own countries by bringing their capital home from abroad. Foreign direct investment cannot be expected to return to Central America if domestic investors stay away. To attract either domestic or foreign investors, governments will have to promote private-sector-oriented policies aggressively. And opposition parties will have to be generally supportive. Investors will be taking a long view of their options in Central America.

In this regard, it is encouraging to learn of the number of émigrés who returned to their home countries with the savings from several years of working in the United States. These small entrepreneurs may be the forerunners of the modernization of business practice in the region.

The Social Debt

The poor have borne the brunt of the 1980s crisis, and, if Central America is to achieve competitive integration into the world market, countries must address the social issues with urgency. The statistics of poverty cited above are already a compelling reason. But there are also economic arguments. On the one hand, to compete in the international marketplace, Central American producers will have both to learn and apply the latest technologies. To do so, workers will need to be educated and trained, and, to be able to be educated and trained, they will need to enjoy a minimum stability and quality of life. On the other hand, if regional integration is to work and the regional market is to become a motor of development, the population of the region will have to have incomes with which to purchase regionally produced goods. The World Bank cites appealing percentages of school-aged children matriculating in primary level education in Central America. The numbers range from 70 percent to 97 percent, but secondary education enrollments fall by one-half. In either case, enrollments do not equal graduates. Similarly, calorie supply per capita in Central America parallels that of low-income countries, not middle- or lower middle-income countries.

Political Stabilization

Perhaps the most important step toward stabilizing the political environment in Central America would be ending guerrilla activity in the region. Following that, prompt demobilization of the military is called for. In the absence of internal war, the Central American countries do not require a standing armed force. President Oscar Arias has called on the countries of the region to follow the Costa Rican model of democracy with armed forces replaced by an all-purpose, well-trained constabulary. U.S. assistance to administration of justice programs in the past several years is to be commended. It is extremely heartening to hear Salvadorans discussing these options.

Even with demobilization, however, the political equation in Central America is very fragile. In particular, institutional capabilities are extremely poor or nonexistent. Major efforts must be devoted to developing minimal capabilities in public bureaucracies. Justice systems must be developed and financed. Regulations and the rules of the game that make an economic climate attractive to investors need to be revised and made transparent. Governments must very obviously endorse social equity. As Minister Pedro Aspe of Mexico notes, "We don't want a rich Mexico and poor Mexicans." In many cases, intense efforts today will only have demonstrable results a generation from now. Donors will have to be patient.

Who Will Pay?

As the debate over economic policy in Latin America evolves, more reflective and analytic postures are replacing the dependencista arguments of yesterday that too often placed blame for the region's failed performance almost exclusively on external factors. Increasingly Latin Americans are borrowing Pogo's observation: "We have met the enemy and they are us." Notwithstanding this healthy introspective trend, Central America in particular will have to rely greatly on the external community for resources to rebuild their economies.

The principal sources of development financing will be the IDB, the World Bank, the U.S. government, and other bilateral agencies in Europe, Japan, and Latin America itself. Historically, the IDB has been the development bank for Central America. IDB lending has been approximately double that of the World Bank in recent years. While the

World Bank will take a more active role in the near future, especially in adjustment lending, which it will undertake with the IDB, under the IDB's seventh replenishment, it must spend 35 percent of its $22.5 billion lending program in the so-called C and D countries (Costa Rica is a C country; the others are D countries—the least well-off countries). That target represents a major challenge to the Bank and to its Central American members. In the current two-year pipeline project, only 15 percent of projects identified are targeted at the D countries and 7 percent at the Cs. There will be inevitable delays in developing an investment program capable of addressing national and regional needs.

More important, IDB project financing requires a substantial counterpart investment by the borrowing country and such counterparts have been, and may continue to be, difficult to generate from government budgets that will necessarily be squeezed from many corners. In the case of the poorest Central American countries, they must put up 20 percent of project costs, or, in certain situations in which more than 50 percent of the beneficiaries are poor, the country's component may be reduced to 10 percent. Other obstacles must also be overcome. Central American countries have serious problems in both developing "bankable" projects and in implementing them in a timely fashion. The institutional weaknesses of government agencies must be addressed promptly and aggressively, but it would be wishful thinking to believe that they will be rapidly overcome.

Timing of Assistance

The Kissinger Commission recommended approximately $8 billion in five years to five Central American countries. The Sanford Commission more recently recommended $2 billion per year for five years, including $850 million in concessional funds. In the very short term, bilateral agencies will have to cover the financial gaps, for charter restrictions preclude lending to countries that are in arrears as are Honduras, Nicaragua, and Panama.

Almost every commission studying the Central American crisis has recommended consultation and coordination among donors. Both the Kissinger Commission and the Sanford Commission recommended that the IDB assume responsibility for this function. At present, the United Nations Development Program has acquired the task, and will continue to be an important player in providing technical assistance to the region. Because of its longer experience in the Caribbean context, its experience in bilateral donor consultations by its staff of economic experts, and its critical involvement in adjustment as well as project lending, in addition to technical assistance, the World Bank has assumed the task of coordinating country-level assistance. The Inter-American Development Bank will play a similar role in regional integration. Finally, recognizing that coordinating assistance from all sources and planning its efficient application in the region is one of the biggest development tasks, Secretary Baker has proposed a G-24 mechanism patterned after the mechanism developed for Eastern Europe.

Regardless of which agency assumes the responsibility, serious efforts must begin immediately with both a bilateral and regional orientation. The region's requirements are greater than all the resources available to deal with them. Yet, the resources presently available could also overwhelm the fragile economies and leave them permanently dependent on external largesse. Central American development will take time, careful planning and programming, serious commitment on the part of its own leaderships, patience on the part of its people, and lots of good luck.

CEPAL claimed in 1986 with respect to the style of development in Central America that a "noteworthy feature is that, in the thirty years since the end of the Second World War, most of the considerable changes undergone by the economies of the region have been simply superimposed on the economic and social structure that already existed, without bringing about any essential changes in it." In 1969 Luigi Einaudi edited a book that he entitled, "Latin Americans Take Charge of their Future." Subsequent events have proved that title premature—certainly in the case of Central America. But, perhaps, now is the time for Central Americans to take charge of their future.

JUAN VINCENTE MALDONADO

The Role of the Private Sector in Economic Development

During the last decade, there has been a poor record of economic de-velopment and growth in Central America. Presently, most Central American nations face the challenge of reactivating their economies and reducing their poverty levels to satisfy the basic needs of their populations, which is necessary for stable government.

THE NEED FOR A NEW ECONOMIC AND SOCIAL STRATEGY FOR THE REGION

The figures in table 1 illustrate that, with the exception of Costa Rica, all the other Central American countries are far from achieving the macroeconomic goal of growth with stability. Per capita growth is low for most Central American nations and negative for Nicaragua. Open unemployment is above 10 percent in Guatemala and above 20 per-cent in El Salvador, Honduras, and Nicaragua. The inflation rate is about 17 percent for Costa Rica, El Salvador, Guatemala, and Hondu-ras, and has reached hyperinflation levels in Nicaragua. The poor re-cord of growth is accompanied by serious internal and external dis-equilibrium that is being financed with foreign aid, which will ultimately hurt these countries because of negative dependency re-percussions.

Central American countries are in the process, some more ad-vanced than others, of adjusting their economic strategies to a more efficient and intensive use of the markets as the determining factor in allocating services and resources. This would involve a rediscovery and a recognition of the basic economic principles of a free-market economy—private property, competition, and a new role for the state and the private sector in development strategy.

TABLE 1. *Basic Economic Indicators in Five Central American Countries,*
1983–89

Indicator and Country	1983	1984	1985	1986	1987	1988	1989
Real GNP (percent change)							
Costa Rica	2.9	8.0	0.7	5.5	5.4	3.8	5.0
El Salvador	0.8	2.3	2.0	0.6	2.7	0.5	0.9
Guatemala	−2.6	0.5	−0.6	0.1	3.1	3.5	4.0
Honduras	−0.2	2.8	3.2	3.1	4.9	4.0	2.5
Nicaragua	4.6	−1.6	−4.1	−1.0	−1.1	−8.3	−3.0
Per capita GNP (percent change)							
Costa Rica	−0.1	4.9	−2.0	2.7	2.7	1.1	2.3
El Salvador	−0.3	1.4	0.7	−1.1	0.9	−6.0	−0.9
Guatemala	−5.2	−2.3	−3.7	−2.2	0.4	0.8	0.8
Honduras	−3.2	−0.1	0.2	0.2	2.0	1.6	n.a.
Nicaragua	1.4	−4.9	−7.3	−4.3	−4.5	−11.4	−6.4
Open unemployment (percent)							
Costa Rica	7.9	6.7	6.2	6.1	5.5	5.6	3.8
El Salvador	32.9	32.2	23.8	24.0	24.5	24.0	n.a.
Guatemala	11.0	10.0	13.7	16.6	12.6	12.6	n.a.
Honduras	21.0	21.0	22.0	23.0	24.0	24.0	n.a.
Nicaragua	19.0	21.1	20.9	22.1	24.3	26.0	n.a.
Inflation rate (percent change)							
Costa Rica	32.6	11.9	15.9	11.8	16.8	20.8	16.7
El Salvador	13.1	11.7	22.3	31.9	24.9	19.8	17.6
Guatemala	6.4	3.4	18.7	36.9	12.3	10.8	n.a.
Honduras	8.3	4.7	3.4	4.4	2.5	4.5	n.a.
Nicaragua	31.0	35.4	219.5	681.6	1,011.9	14,315.8	n.a.
Current account balance (percent of GNP)							
Costa Rica	−9.1	−4.2	−3.3	−1.8	−5.7	−3.0	−7.3
El Salvador	−0.9	−1.6	−0.9	3.4	3.0	1.1	3.5
Guatemala	−2.5	−4.1	−3.7	−0.3	−6.2	−5.9	n.a.
Honduras	−7.3	9.8	−5.9	−3.9	−5.5	−5.2	n.a.
Nicaragua	−21.1	22.6	−30.6	−28.0	−24.8	−23.2	−21.6

Source: Data from the Economic Commission for Latin America and the Caribbean
(CEPAL).
   n.a. Not available.

A free-market economy will also demand a total commitment to the principles of democracy and justice. The real benefits of a free-market system can be better achieved in a society where democratic institutions exist because of the convictions of its members. This, together with a sound system for administering justice, constitutes two solid areas in which real economic and social development can be achieved. To achieve development there is a need to establish conditions to reduce extreme poverty, use the scarce resources available in a more efficient way, create a new revolutionary social strategy, and give a "true" recognition to the private sector.

Most Central American countries face the necessity for short-term economic adjustment to reorganize their levels of expenditures to their real income levels. At the same time, they confront the need to start an intense process of structural adjustments that involves relative price changes, institutional adjustments, opening the economies to facilitate use of the external sector as the engine of growth, liberalizing the markets and allowing prices to give the proper signals to economic agents, reducing the public bureaucracies, changing and reorienting subsidies to the poor, eliminating privileges, and many other economic measures that will tend to shake the structure of the Central American economies.

A new and revolutionary social strategy requires a complete reorientation of the procedure through which the social problem has been handled in the past. The problem is more one of absolute than relative poverty, which means an entire redefinition of the social strategy by exerting most of the effort on reorienting the expenditures of the public sector and granting subsidies to the poor.

To achieve success in this endeavor, all of the public social sectors must be reformed, starting with decentralizing public services in education, health and nutrition, employment programs, and many others. These changes are now beginning in El Salvador and Honduras and will soon take place in Guatemala and Nicaragua. Costa Rica has had a more stable record of economic and social development and is now in the process of adjusting its fiscal accounts. All of these adjustment programs could be supported by international institutions such as the World Bank, the IMF, IDB, and AID.

The Role of the Private Sector

The most important question involves the role of the private sector in this process. It appears that the private sector can take one of two possible approaches—either a passive or an active role. The passive approach consists in merely responding to the new set of incentives given by the new strategies.

This role can be played with a negative attitude and short-term point of view or with a positive attitude and long-term perspective. It is clear that some sectors are going to suffer in the process of adjustment as a result of tariff and tax reform, such as the elimination of exemptions and loopholes. The negative attitude and short-term approach induces the private sector to engage in an internal battle, with everyone trying to defend his own interests. A typical argument with this approach would be: "It is fine to liberate the markets but not the market I have to deal with." The positive attitude and long-term approach requires a better understanding of the process because this is not a zero-sum game. In other words, this approach offers the opportunity for a process of adjustment in which everyone is going to gain and to work.

In view of this, it is tempting to suggest the passive role with a positive attitude and long-term perspective. Nevertheless, it is apparent that this approach is absolutely inadequate given the challenges faced by the Central American countries. The private sector should assume a more active role, which is far more demanding.

The Challenge of an Active Role in the Process of Economic Adjustment and Social Development

Undoubtedly, in Central America and in many other developing countries of the world, most intellectual and entrepreneurial capacities are in the private sector of the economies. It is also true that the private sector will fulfill most of its "social responsibilities" by producing and maximizing profits. In this manner, jobs are created, new technology is developed, quality products and services are produced, and investment and societies' welfare are increased. This is not true if profits in one sector are achieved at the expense of another, which would be the result of a distorted economic system. Assuming what was said previously, Central American countries will move toward a less distorted economic system in which the private sector will concentrate on its only role—production of goods and services.

The problem is that, although this role is valid in more developed societies, it is insufficient in Central America because it assumes that a process of change from the present economic and social system to the new system will result regardless of the attitude and role of the private sector. This cannot be true for one simple reason: in the political, cultural, military, religious, and economic life of these countries the sole agent of change in the direction of a free market is the private sector. The other sectors generally are committed to other causes and interests. The thesis of this chapter is that the private sector must be the protagonist of the process of change. Without its dynamic and active role, the change is not going to be possible regardless of the efforts and intellectual capacity of the politicians in government. For this strategy to be successful, the private sector must undertake the following tasks: the self-education and dissemination of ideas and the generation of applied research, which is needed for the successful implementation of economic and social reforms; the demonstration through pilot economic projects that the new strategy works; and the involvement in the execution of social projects to demonstrate the viability of the new social strategy.

Self-Education and Dissemination of Ideas

One of the most important barriers for any process of economic reforms is that most people do not understand either the reason that the change is needed or of what it consists. Moreover, there is much misunderstanding about what constitutes a free-market economic system. Imposing such a system by decree will not work in countries in which new democratic liberties have recently been established. It is not easy for the private sector to undertake this task because it is also beset by confusion. In many countries, the private sector has founded private think tanks to do this job. The problem is that the challenge is not merely having a think tank but actively involving the private-sector leaders in the think tanks. The risk is that the private sector limits itself only to the creation of the think tank without further involvement. In this case, the participation of the private sector is only a passive one, and the education process of the private entrepreneurs, which is crucial for the process of change, is not achieved.

In many cases, think tanks are managed by the intellectuals who produce reliable economic analysis but maintain little communication with the private-sector leaders.

Considering the lack of understanding in Central America of the basic principles of a free-market economic system and that, in the last thirty years, the efforts of most of the intellectuals have been oriented toward promoting an economic system based on government intervention and central planning, it is crucial for the private sector to start a process of educating itself if it ever wants to participate.

The experience of FUSADES in El Salvador is very interesting in this respect. FUSADES was started with the sole intention of creating an economic and social think tank. But, it was not just a matter of hiring the right people and funding their work. The involvement of FUSADES founders, all of whom were private entrepreneurs, was crucial. Committees worked on fiscal matters, financial and monetary policy, social strategies, and so on. This was the core of the work of the Economic and Social Studies Department of the institution. In this way, a very productive relationship was introduced between the entrepreneurs, who had many years of practical experience in different areas, and the professional economists, who had a clear theoretical base in economics. A two-way process of education began. There are now entrepreneurs and professional economists in political positions as members of the economic cabinet, and, through their working experience in FUSADES, they have learned to communicate with one another in the same language.

During the last five years, FUSADES, as a think tank, has played an important role in educating businessmen, politicians, media people, the military, and people in the labor sector by teaching them free-market principles. The private sector must participate in disseminating the principles and ideas that constitute the basis of a free-market economic system. This is a long-term process. It is true that there are other institutions, such as universities, that can assume this responsibility. The problem in Central America is that most of the universities are almost exclusively devoted to teaching, and some of them are too involved in politics to function properly.

The basic principles of a free-market economy, such as property rights, equity and justice, profits, and competition are very obscure for most of the population. The process of change from an inefficient, distorted, corrupted, and interventionist economic system to another where most of the responsibilities are given to the individuals becomes easier in direct proportion to the economic education of the population. It is very important to improve the private sector's image in the region, which can be achieved if the private sector is committed to this process of change and participates actively in all the different phases of the process.

The Task of Opening Foreign Markets and Attracting Investors

The new economic system for the region must give the external sector priority consideration. When the new model was presented, many people asked "But, What are we going to export?" Behind this concern is the fear that the countries are poor in natural resources without natural advantages. The question also reflects skepticism about what the private energies can achieve when they are guided by the proper economic incentives and signals.

The new economic system calls for export expansion. The private sector can play an important role with the government by institutionalizing an export promotion strategy, introducing new technology and adapting it to local needs to achieve a diversification of production capacity with export potential, promoting investment by locals and foreigners, assisting small entrepreneurs in the process of adjusting to the new and more competitive environment, raising quality concerns among local producers, and many other similar issues.

A successful export-oriented strategy must be based on the proper macroeconomic setting and on a change of "mentality" among private entrepreneurs. This is not easy to achieve when the private sector is familiar with a closed economy where the rent-seeking process is linked to bureaucratic favors and loopholes resulting from state intervention. The private sector must be the first to acknowledge that the system is going to change and act accordingly.

There are many experiences around the world where strong cooperation between the government and the private sector has been crucial in the export expansion strategy. The government bureaucracy alone is not prepared to do the job that is required. We are aware of two relevant experiences in Central America. One is in Costa Rica, where the private sector and the government have been promoting foreign investment and helping private entrepreneurs in the process of developing foreign markets for its products. The other is in El Salvador, where similar efforts are under way.

Most Central American countries are heavily dependent upon agriculture. Their economic recovery depends on the recovery and health of the agricultural sector. Many natural and relative advantages rely directly or indirectly on this sector. Technology and product diversification are crucial to agricultural development. The private sector can play an important role either alone or in cooperation with the government. Again, an example is the case of El Salvador, where efforts are being made to plant new crops of fruits and vegetables that are now starting to be exported.

Apart from these innovative endeavors, the private sector in many Central American countries must be prepared to assume managerial responsibilities in many areas that were nationalized in the last decade. This is the case in the banking sector and the external trade of export products such as coffee and sugar in El Salvador. It is important to note that the private sector must assume the responsibilities that this privatization process demands, and must adequately respond to the expectations that come with the rights and responsibilities demanded by a free-market system.

The Social Strategy: Participation of the Private Sector

The elimination of the extreme poverty in the region is not solely a responsibility of the state. More important, it is a responsibility of each and every one of the inhabitants, including the poor. The new social strategy must complement economic strategy and requires an intense participation of the private sector in implementing the social programs. The state has not been able to tackle the poverty dilemma alone, and has created a huge bureaucracy that increasingly absorbs more resources that could be used for the programs. This is true of the ministries of education and health in most countries of the region.

An important element of the new social strategy is the decentralization of the social programs using intermediate organizations such as municipalities and private organizations. The private sector has much to do in many of the social sectors. One example is technical education, where there is no doubt that the private chambers (industry, agriculture, and others) are the ones that are better aware of their needs. It is also possible to think of the private sector participating in primary education and in higher education as well. This requires a new way of reorienting the public resources to these programs, such as giving subsidies to each student who has been attending school.

Once again, the experience in El Salvador can be cited. There is a private institution devoted to the development of education, another to housing, and a third looks after the prevention of occupational risks.

A common denominator among all of these institutions is the intense involvement of private entrepreneurs in them. It is important to distinguish between merely contributing money and becoming personally involved in managing the social programs. The private sector's involvement in social programs gives them another dimension and contributes to changing the image of just being the "selfish profit maximizers."

Through these actions of disseminating economic principles and participating in social programs, the private sector is demonstrating that the new strategy of economic and social development is feasible. The private sector must actively participate by leading this process of change.

Is the Private Sector Prepared for the Active Role?

As previously mentioned, there are several examples in the region that reveal this kind of attitude. Even more important, those changes have occurred in the midst of situations that did not at all promote this kind of behavior.

What is being suggested is a private sector effort toward a supranational intersectoral interest, such as linking the promotion of education and the fight against illiteracy with a good administration of justice and a sound export-oriented policy. For this purpose, it is much more effective to combine individual efforts than company efforts. In other words, private entrepreneurs must get involved on a more personal level.

The risk that exists and that can hinder this active role is the faulty perception of some members of the private sector that with the recent political movements to more conservative governments in the region (as in the case of El Salvador, Honduras, Costa Rica, and Nicaragua), their involvement in the discussion of public policy has become less important. Even worse than that could be the attitude that considers the new governments as governments of and for the private sector.

It has to be crystal clear that, in general, economic policy is always society-oriented with social welfare as a necessary part of the maximizing function. The private sector will have to pay the price in the short-term adjustment process (less access to subsidized credit, elimination of tax exemptions, and so on) and will also have to pay all the cost associated with the economic structural reforms.

The revitalization of the private sector in the region should not come with more subsidies and privileges. On the contrary, it should emerge from more efficient and clearly defined rules of the game and from taking advantage of all the spaces that the governments will open when it adopts its "proper" role within a free-market economy. For this economic strategy to survive, the private sector of Central America must become the real agent of change and must be more dynamic and vital than in the past, leading the way with its involvement toward better and more equitable societies.

RICHARD L. MILLETT

Unequal Partners: Relations between the Government and the Military

In 1982, while writing about the political role of Central America's armed forces, Thomas P. Anderson observed:

> Political power became concentrated in their hands and the proud landholder had to receive the military upstart as a temporary social equal. The military, controlling the government, lavished money upon itself for every conceivable purpose except paying the poor, conscripted peasants who served in the ranks. Its pride in professionalism grew and stepped outside the bounds of mere military tactics and strategy to include the murkier realms of higher finance, jurisprudence, and business management. Thus, what has been referred to as "the illusion of military omnipotence" grew, the soldier actually feeling a sort of contempt for the civilian expert. If there should be any doubt about the right of the officer class to rule, such doubts could be removed with the rumble of a few tanks through the streets of the capital. Power grew out of the barrel of a gun.[1]

Outside Costa Rica, this was, until recently, the prevailing view of civil-military relations in Central America. The establishment of a Marxist government in Nicaragua broke the pattern in that nation, which made the armed forces the instrument of the ruling party, rather than the arbiter of the political process. The victory of the UNO coalition, headed by Violeta Barrios de Chamorro, in the 1990 elections has further complicated this situation because the army officer corps remains tied to the Sandinista National Liberation Front (FSLN), which is now the opposition party. In Panama, the December 1989 intervention virtually destroyed the higher officer corps of the old Panamanian Defense Force (PDF), but creating a successor force

1. Thomas P. Anderson, *Politics in Central America* (Praeger, 1982), p. 195.

has proved to be both difficult and controversial. In El Salvador, Guatemala, and Honduras, the military's independence of and, at times, dominance over civilian authorities continue, and civil-military relations have been characterized more by conflict than by cooperation. In recent years, however, there are indications that this situation is beginning to change. Civilian governments have been installed in all three nations, and there have been no coups for over six years. Human rights violations by the armed forces remain a serious problem, especially in El Salvador and Guatemala, but they are below the level of the early 1980s. Higher officers regularly issue statements of support for elected, democratic government. What has not changed, however, is the determination of the military to maintain its autonomy, to resist any effort to allow civilians to control internal military affairs, to dictate internal security policy, or to make officers subject to the judgment of civil courts.

Although traditional patterns of civil-military relations appear to be breaking down, this has not eliminated, nor even greatly reduced, the tensions present in these relations. In some ways the situation is more strained today than previously. Even the armed forces are increasingly divided over the question of their role in society and the extent to which they should allow civilians to exercise effective political power. Civilians, in turn, are reevaluating relations with the military. Those on the far Right, no longer able to depend upon strong military support, have become more willing to criticize the armed forces, while those on the Left seem increasingly flexible in their approaches to the military institution. Complicating the situation is the continuing regional political violence, which threatens the survival of both civil and military institutions.

HISTORICAL CONTEXT

The roots of current patterns of civil-military relations in El Salvador, Guatemala, and Honduras began during Spanish colonial rule. Under Spanish rule, the military was

> . . . a class apart and so regarded itself. The possession of special privileges enhanced its sense of uniqueness and superiority, and at the same time rendered it virtually immune from civil author-

ity. Unfortunately, power and privilege were not accompanied by a commensurate sense of responsibility. A large proportion of officers and men regarded military service as an opportunity for the advancement of personal interests rather than as a civil obligation.[2]

These attitudes and habits were inherited by postindependence armies that also added major new elements to the pattern of civil-military relations. During the first fifty years of independence, Central American armed forces became both the servants of competing political factions, Liberal and Conservative, and the instruments of individual military strongmen, military caudillos, individuals who "resorted to martial solutions in regulating the morality of the inhabitants, suppressing criticism of their own policies, and persecuting their enemies."[3]

In Guatemala and El Salvador this pattern began to change during the last third of the nineteenth century. "Liberal" dictators took power in both nations, determined to establish order and accelerate the pace of national development. This agenda necessitated the creation of more modern, professional armies. Foreign instructors were brought in, military academies were established, and new equipment was purchased. These efforts produced two basic alterations in the traditional political equation. The first was the creation of professional, career officers, who were capable of developing interests separate from, and acting independently of, existing political factions. The other was the exacerbation of the power imbalance between the military and civilians. The military became the most modernized and most institutionalized sector of society, giving it the capacity to act independently of traditional political leadership. It also increasingly combined police and military functions, giving it a virtual monopoly over the use of armed force.

By the 1960s, a new pattern of civil-military relations was emerging in Central America—a pattern that continues to influence the region. An increasingly institutionalized military had become the ultimate arbiter or political power. Outside Nicaragua, the armed forces were no longer faithful instruments of a single individual or family. Generals might become presidents, but they were likely to be removed from

2. Lyle McCalister, *The Fuero Militar in New Spain* (University of Florida Press, 1957), p. 15.
3. Ralph Lee Woodward, Jr., *Central America: A Nation Divided* (Oxford University Press, 1985), 2d ed., pp. 103–104.

office, or at least prevented from extending their time in power, by the military. Political parties increasingly found military support more important than popular support in gaining and maintaining power. On both sides, the perceived gap between officers and civilians, which had always been significant, increased, and, in cases of conflict, the United States was often perceived as supporting the military.

In the area of human rights an especially significant change occurred. The military began to target, or at least permit to be targeted, individuals on the basis of their ideology rather than their actions. This trend was encouraged and promoted by extreme Right civilian factions who portrayed their opponents as advocating programs that threatened the power, privileges, and even the survival, of the military institution. The growing involvement of the military with the police, especially in El Salvador, but also in Honduras and Guatemala, exacerbated this problem, making it virtually impossible to separate the military high command from the abuses perpetrated by police and other internal security forces.

As the political power of the military grew, so did its influence on the economy. One aspect of this was U.S.-promoted involvement of armed forces in civic action programs. Development became linked with national security and counterinsurgency. At the same time, officers began to profit, both individually and institutionally, from their increased political power. Both active-duty and retired officers began to enter into business activities, using military connections and privileges to procure advantages not available to their civilian competitors. This led some civilians to seek partnership arrangements with officers, while other businessmen became increasingly critical and resentful of the military's economic role. While at its worst in pre-1979 Nicaragua, this situation was a growing problem throughout the region.

Civilian institutions also underwent basic changes in the 1960s and 1970s. The expanded middle class and rising educational levels led to the development of political parties—notably Christian Democratic and Social Democratic—based on ideology rather than traditional personal or regional loyalties. These parties had ties outside the region, notably in Europe and in South America, which gave them access to resources hitherto unavailable to Central American political parties. Labor, too, despite frequent attempts at repression, was becoming organized and was developing international contacts. Of at least equal significance was the organization during this period of national business, industrial, and commercial organizations, which provided more unified and effective forums for articulating and promoting the interests of the private sector.

The net effect of these changes was dual. First, the relative institutional advantage that the military had enjoyed since early in the century vis à vis civilian institutions began to diminish. The armed forces were still the most powerful and cohesive institution in each nation, but their ability to dominate the system was declining, and the number of ever-strengthened competing civilian institutions was expanding. At the same time, there was a rapid increase in both the numbers and potential power of civilian sectors that were unhappy with the current status of society and the prevailing pattern of civil-military relations.

Both military and civilian institutions responded to these changes in various ways. Beginning in the 1960s, officers began to insert themselves more directly into partisan politics, either through alliances with civilian sectors or through forming parties that were essentially instruments of the armed forces. Military incursions into party politics ultimately proved unsuccessful. Military-backed parties were unable to attract a mass following, and parties such as the National Party in Honduras or the Revolutionary Democratic Party (PRD) in Panama, which allowed themselves to become vehicles for the armed forces, were faced with a public backlash. The armed forces found it impossible to maintain independence of civil authority and accountability while simultaneously developing a mass political base through which they could control that authority. Their political allies tended to be opportunists, extreme Right factions, and, most frequently, upper- and middle-rank bureaucrats. These bureaucrats, who often owed their positions to the military and operated "in a similar organizational milieu," tended "to see the world in a somewhat similar way."[4] But these groups were never able to coalesce into an effective unit nor extend their appeal to the society as a whole. Instead, they had to resort to manipulation, intimidation, and fraud to maintain power. Military-created parties are

. . . unable to hold the masses because the coalition essential to maintain the working of the polity at any level does not permit

4. Edward Feit, *The Armed Bureaucrats* (Houghton Mifflin, 1973), p. 11.

regenerative changes to be made. Thus the hollowness of the ritual sooner or later becomes evident, destroying whatever of a mass following the military regime may have had. The military regime fails because it can neither hold together the disparate and hostile social forces it has had to harness, nor maintain the mass support that, through organizational analogy, it might otherwise have held.[5]

Central America's military regimes were badly shaken by a series of external events during the latter half of the 1970s. The first of these was the advent of the Carter administration, which emphasized human rights and opposed military governments. More serious was the downturn in the regional economy during the late 1970s. The final, and, perhaps, most significant, factor was the fall of the Somoza regime in Nicaragua at the hands of the Marxist guerrillas of the FSLN. During the upheaval, the Nicaraguan military institution was destroyed, which caused widespread consternation among the officer corps in other Central American nations.

Internal violence soon began mounting rapidly in El Salvador, Guatemala, and, after 1982, in Nicaragua. Insurgent movements were expanding, and urban terrorism was increasing. In El Salvador and Guatemala, death squads and private right-wing armies were escalating their activities, usually with covert military backing. By the fall of 1979, El Salvador appeared to be on the verge of major civil conflict, and Guatemala was not far behind.

Each nation's military reacted to the crisis in a distinct way. In Honduras, the army moved to rebuild relations with both the United States and the traditional political parties by beginning a slow, but steady, process of return to civilian rule. In Guatemala, the regime of General Romeo Lucas Garcia attempted to increase its control and defy its foes. The alliance between the military and all but the extreme Right faction of the political spectrum was broken. Political and labor leaders were assassinated and Vice-President Francisco Villagran Kramer had to flee into exile after publicly observing that "death or exile is the fate of those who struggle for justice in Guatemala."[6] In El Sal-

5. Feit, *Armed Bureaucrats*, p. 19.
6. Richard Millett, "The United States and Central America," in *The Political Economy of the Western Hemisphere: Selected Issues for U.S. Policy*, Selected Essays Prepared for the Use of the Committee on International Trade, Finance, and

vador, the regime of General Carlos Humberto Romero vacillated between brutal repression and efforts to open contacts with the United States. On October 15, 1979, with at least the tacit blessing of the United States, a coup by junior officers ousted Romero and installed a mixed civilian-military junta.

DEVELOPMENTS IN THE 1980S

The October 15 coup produced a significant break in the pattern of civil-military relations. Direct military involvement in politics and the separation from, and hostility toward, the civilian population, which had been common in previous decades, now threatened rather than promoted the interests of the military institution. While still extremely suspicious of politicians on the Left, many officers were becoming disillusioned with those on the extreme Right. Mounting insurgency threats, combined with serious problems in acquiring and maintaining modern equipment, made it desirable to renew or strengthen ties with the United States, which would be virtually impossible without an improvement in the human rights situation.

Many civilians also found cause for seeking improved civil-military relations. The political center, often persecuted by, and, consequently, hostile to, the military, now found itself threatened by the rise of the armed Left. Business groups witnessed mounting violence destroying their investments, decimating their profits, and imperiling their economic future. Suspicions were high, levels of mutual confidence extremely low, and many officers and civilians remained committed to preservation of the status quo, but, despite such barriers, significant alterations in civil-military relations began to occur.

In El Salvador, in particular, obstacles to the reshaping of relations have been powerful and unrelenting. On the military side, these include the long history of abuses committed against the civilian population, the lack of any tradition of holding officers accountable for such abuses, high levels of internal corruption, and, most important, the overwhelming influence of the *tanda* system—the tendency of officers to give almost total support and protection to those who graduated from the nation's military academy in their class or *tanda*. Alli-

Security Economics of the Joint Economic Committee, 97 Cong. 1 sess. (Government Printing Office, 1981), pp. 22–23.

ances are formed between *tandas,* and an officer's career depends as much on the success of his *tanda* as it does on his own ability.[7]

On the civilian side, obstacles include a heritage of distrust of, and sometimes near contempt for, the military; the high level of political polarization, with significant elements on both Right and Left opposed to the establishment of a democratic system; and, as in the military, high levels of corruption and overweening personal ambition. Finally, for both civilians and military, the ongoing insurgency and the declining economy made reforms even more difficult, and increased the temptation to seek violent solutions.

Some progress in civilian control over the military appeared to occur during the mid-1980s. The military adopted an essentially neutral position during the 1984 presidential and 1985 legislative elections, which allowed the Christian Democrats to win. Death squad activities were curbed, although no one involved in such activities was arrested and convicted for past actions. The real balance of power became clear when authorities uncovered a kidnapping ring run by military officers posing as left-wing guerrillas. This ring extorted over $4 million from wealthy Salvadoran businessmen. Although at least one officer who was involved was dismissed from the army, and others were briefly arrested, no one was convicted. Significantly, the key officer who was implicated, Lt. Col. Roberto Mauricio Staben, was released and returned to duty.[8] He remained in key commands until May 1990, when he was sent to Honduras as military attaché.

The fiasco of the kidnapping-ring investigations signaled a halt to the progress made in civil-military relations. The balance of power within the military was changing; power was falling into the hands of the officers who graduated in the class of 1966. Known as the *tandona* because of its large size, its members have closer links to ARENA than to the Christian Democrats.

Since 1987, the military has been increasingly outspoken, although not fully united, on issues of politics and of civil-military relations, and it appears to be increasingly disenchanted with civilian politicians. In May 1988, Col. Emilio Ponce, who was soon to replace Gen-

7. Brook Larmer, "The Shifting Battle-front," *Christian Science Monitor,* October 20, 1988, pp. 16–17; and Lt. Col. A. J. Bacevich and others, "American Military Policy in Small Wars: The Case of El Salvador," paper prepared for presentation at the Kennedy School of Government, Harvard University, March 1988, p. 47.

8. Americas Watch Committee, *The Civilian Toll, 1986–87: Ninth Supplement to the Report on Human Rights in El Salvador* (New York, 1987), pp. 237–244.

eral Blandon as Chairman of the Armed Forces Joint Chiefs of Staff—
a position second in power to that of the Defense Minister—declared
that politicians' "individualistic attitude and lack of political maturity
is putting into jeopardy the constitutionality of the country." Another
colonel added that "politicians weren't given the vote so they could
use politics for their own personal ends, but to make laws to govern
the country."[9]

The inauguration in 1989 of an ARENA government, headed by
President Alfredo Cristiani, also seemed likely to reduce tensions between civil and military authorities. This changed, however, with the
November 1989 murder of six prominent Jesuit priests who were associated with El Salvador's Catholic university. Massive evidence
emerged of high-level military complicity in these murders—notably
Colonel Guillermo Alfredo Benavides, a member of the *tandona*. Key
evidence has been destroyed, however, and hopes for a successful
prosecution of those involved have steadily declined.[10] The result has
been increased criticism of El Salvador's military in the United States,
which presents the possibility of a major reduction in military assistance. It has also produced divisions within the armed forces; both
retired and active duty officers have condemned the crime and criti-
cized aspects of the investigation.[11] The ultimate resolution of this
case will be a key indication of the future evolution of civil-military
relations.

In Guatemala, the bloody rule of General Lucas was ended in 1982,
when junior officers installed a military junta, headed by retired General Efrain Rios Montt. The general, an aggressive evangelical, had
little use for politicians on either the Left or Right, for insurgents, for
human rights groups, or for the Roman Catholic Church. Rios Montt
tried to curb military corruption, and lectured officers on their con-
duct. His evangelical fervor alienated many, and his violations of
principles of military hierarchy upset senior officers. In August 1983,
the Minister of Defense, General Oscar Humberto Mejia Victores,
ousted Rios Montt and installed himself as Chief of State.

9. *Christian Science Monitor*, May 11, 1988, p. 10.
10. For a summary of the crime and subsequent investigation, see Con-
gressman Joe Moakley and others, *Interim Report of the Speakers Task Force on El
Salvador*, April 30, 1990.
11. Foreign Broadcast Information Service (FBIS), May 10, 1990, pp. 13–14;
May 21, 1990, pp. 13–14; May 29, 1990, pp. 6–8; and June 11, 1990, pp. 19–21.

General Mejia Victores soon made it clear that he was determined to restore civilian government. In 1984 a Constituent Assembly was elected, and presidential and congressional elections were held in 1985. For various reasons, the military abandoned its traditional position and allowed a relatively open election, which resulted in a sweeping victory for the Christian Democrats (DCG), who were led by Vinicio Cerezo. This course of events was partly a result of efforts by Cerezo to convince the military that he represented no threat to the institution. It also reflected a belief that the DCG could secure desperately needed economic and military assistance for Guatemala as well as a realization that electoral fraud would virtually eliminate any prospects for such assistance. Perhaps the most basic factor, however, was growing military disillusionment with politicians of the Right. Many officers felt that they had been used and abused by upper-class elites and their political allies, and thought that, as a result, the institution had suffered heavy loss of life and severe damage to its image and honor.

Although the army was determined to allow Cerezo to take office, it had no intention of allowing him a free exercise of power. As a candidate, Cerezo barely recognized that reality, stating that "I cannot advocate agrarian reform because it would not be tolerated by the military." [12] By his own estimate, he entered office with 30 percent of the power, which he hoped to more than double by the end of his term. [13]

Ties between military and police forces are not nearly so close in Guatemala as in El Salvador or Honduras, which permitted Cerezo a degree of freedom in reforming the police by discharging many of the worst elements. The armed forces, however, would not allow the president to gain total control over this force, because they feared that it might become a counterweight to military influence. In late 1986 the armed forces forced a change in Guatemala's police chief, and in May 1988 military pressure was reportedly responsible for the ouster of Cerezo's interior minister, who exercised control over the police. [14]

The Esquipulas II Agreement created problems in civil-military relations in Guatemala just as they did in El Salvador. When, in conformity with these agreements, the government opened talks with

12. FBIS, June 11, 1990, B 301.
13. Press conference by president-elect Vinicio Cerezo, Carnegie Endowment, Washington, December 1985.
14. *Christian Science Monitor*, March 16, 1987, p. 13.

insurgent representatives, the acting defense minister publicly admitted that many officers were unhappy that such talks were being held and, in public comments, virtually ruled out the possibility of further negotiations.[15] The renewal of talks in 1990 elicited less criticism and even some mildly supportive statements by the military, but there is little reason to believe that military opposition to any major concessions to the guerrillas had decreased.[16]

Efforts of the Cerezo administration to introduce limited tax reforms evoked protests from economic elites, some of whom began to pressure the military to intervene on their behalf. In May 1988, a small group of officers responded by attempting to mount a coup. This failed, largely because the defense minister, General Hector Gramajo, supported the government. Gramajo denounced both civilian and military supporters of the coup attempt. His greatest concern, however, was that the effort represented a break in military unity and discipline, declaring that "because the Army does not accept the discussion of orders by its members, it carried out steps to stop the groups that were advancing towards the capital."[17] The officers who led this effort were dismissed from the armed forces, but were neither imprisoned nor exiled.

Rumors of additional coup attempts, by then aimed as much at Gramajo as at Cerezo, were constant in the months following the abortive May uprising. One officer accused General Gramajo of "being at the service of the Christian Democratic Party instead of protecting the interests of the armed forces."[18] In May 1989, there was another coup attempt, this time involving Air Force officers, but it, too, failed. The general struck back at his opponents; he denounced them as a small, feudal elite with little concern for the nation as a whole, and pledged the support of the armed forces for the democratic process. He also declared that the armed forces would hold members of the military accountable for actions against civilians, pointing to several arrests of enlisted men and lesser disciplinary actions taken against officers.[19]

General Gramajo retired in June 1990, a few months before sched-

15. FBIS, October 16, 1987, p. 5, and October 19, 1987, p. 11.
16. FBIS, May 16, 1990, pp. 19–20.
17. FBIS, May 19, 1988, p. 9.
18. FBIS, September 14, 1988, p. 12.
19. Remarks by General Gramajo delivered at the Miami Editors and Journalists Workshop, April 1989.

uled presidential elections. By then it seemed likely that Cerezo would finish his elected term of office, but it was much less likely that either he or his successor would achieve the 70 percent of power that the president had set as his goal when he took office.

The Guatemalan armed forces appear to have come further than their Salvadoran counterparts in allowing political space for civilians. In some ways this task is easier in Guatemala because of the lower level of insurgency. In an internal publication, the military admitted that its role in earlier years had been that of "an army in occupation of its own country."[20] Recognizing that such a role jeopardizes the institution and its mission to promote national security, the officers seem determined to avoid involvement in partisan politics and to attempt to forge improved relations with civilians at all levels. This does not mean, however, that the army would turn over full power to civilians. As one officer explained: "We made the mistake in the past of trying to be a-political [sic] and this enabled the politicians to manipulate us. What we must be is independent of political parties, exercising supervision over all of them."[21]

At first glance, Honduras seems to have far fewer problems in civil-military relations than its two northern neighbors. It has no active insurgency and only sporadic terrorist incidents. Human rights abuses are a continuing problem, but do not approach the level of those in El Salvador or Guatemala. The military, more or less voluntarily, returned the government to civilians in 1981, and supported free elections in 1985 and in 1989. There are, however, serious problems just below this relatively tranquil surface.

From 1982 until March 1984, while civilian Roberto Suazo Cordova sat in the presidential palace, much greater power was exercised by the Supreme Commander of the Armed Forces, General Gustavo Alvarez Martinez. Armed forces autonomy is ensured by the Honduran Constitution, which gives the civilian government no real control over military appointments, operations, or budgets. The only check on the commander's power is that exercised by the Superior Council of the Armed Forces (CONSUFFAA), which is a body of senior officers created to give voice to institutional interests.

Alvarez used his position to dominate aspects of foreign policy as

20. Ejercito de Guatemala, *Conceptos Doctrinarios de Asuntos Civiles* (Guatemala: n.p., n.d.), p. 8.
21. Confidential interview with Guatemalan officer, 1989.

well as internal security concerns. Virtually ignoring the president, he negotiated directly with the United States on matters concerning the contras, the training of Salvadoran troops in Honduras, and the presence of U.S. forces. A March 1984 internal military coup ousted and exiled Alvarez, and installed Air Force Commander General Walter Lopez Reyes in his place.

With Alvarez ousted, President Suazo now attempted either to extend his own term in office or to ensure the election of an individual he could control. The new supreme commander forged an alliance with peasant, labor, and business groups to block this and to ensure relatively free elections. The result was the 1985 victory of José Azcona Hoyo, a member of the Liberal Party as was Suazo, but a bitter personal rival of the president.

Soon after Azcona's inauguration, General Lopez Reyes was toppled by another internal military coup. The new president was not informed of developments until the ouster was complete, and was given no option other than to accept CONSUFFAA's choice of General Humberto Regalado Hernandez as supreme commander.[22] It was clear to all that the new president had no effective control over the armed forces.

Further infighting plagued the military in subsequent months, and all of it was conducted without any apparent reference to civilian authorities. Meanwhile, the military issued its own pronouncements on matters of internal security and foreign policy, and occasionally publicly lectured civilians, including the president, on their proper roles and duties. In 1989 a power struggle resulted in the replacement of General Regalado as supreme commander, which was another decision that was made with no apparent reference to civilian authority.

Although the government lacks effective control over the armed forces, it does exercise considerable freedom in other areas. Party politics are largely free of military interference, and elections are generally open and honest. Determination of most economic and social policies seems to rest in civilian hands, although both the executive and legislative branches carefully avoid actions that might upset the officers.

Of growing concern are allegations of military involvement in narcotics trafficking. Such accusations strike a tender nerve in the armed

22. Victor Meza, "La Caida de Walter Lopez: Significado y Ensenanzas," *Boletin Informativo Honduras*, no. 58 (Feburary 1986), pp. 1–2.

forces and could potentially disrupt civil-military relations. Respond-ing to press reports of military involvement in narcotics trafficking, General Regalado denounced the reporters for publishing "poison-ous articles," engaging in "cowardly slander," attempting to "ridicule something as sacred for us as the pride in wearing a military uni-form," and spreading "slanders seeking to irresponsibly discredit and tarnish the Armed Forces." According to Regalado, the purpose of such writings was to "destabilize the irreplacable [sic] foundations of the democratic system."[23] The vehemence of the general's denuncia-tions underlined rising tensions in civil-military relations.

It is unclear for how long the uneasy division of power between officers and civilians will endure in Honduras. Rising political vio-lence could jeopardize the situation as could mounting public disillu-sionment with both the armed forces and the political parties. As have its neighbors to the north, Honduras appears to have rejected earlier patterns of civil-military relations and military participation in politics without developing any consistent and effective new pattern.

In Nicaragua and Panama, recent events have created special prob-lems for civil-military relations. Following the successful 1979 revolu-tion by the FSLN, the new army became inextricably linked with the ruling party, not unlike the situation in Cuba. The 1989 electoral vic-tory of the political opposition coalition (UNO), headed by Violeta Barrios de Chamorro, and its assumption of power in early 1990, broke this pattern. Nicaragua now faces the peculiar situation of a civilian government that is headed by one party and a military whose officers are loyal to the chief opposition party. Problems involving the demobilization of the armed opposition, popularly known as the con-tras, further complicates civil-military relations.

The new president decided to retain Humberto Ortega, brother of the former president and a member of the Sandinista Party's ruling directorate, as army commander, though she, herself, took over his previous position as defense minister. This satisfied many Sandinis-tas, but provoked bitter divisions within her own coalition. Vice-President Virgilio Godoy was especially critical and attributed many of the nation's problems to Ortega's retention.[24]

The current status of civil-military relations in Nicaragua is virtu-ally without precedent in Latin America, and its ultimate resolution

23. FBIS, April 20, 1988, p. 9–10.
24. FBIS, May 17, 1990, p. 29.

is impossible to predict. The chance of a coup in the near future seems remote, but the ability of the new government to exercise effective control over the military is still doubtful.

In Panama, the status of civil-military relations deteriorated steadily throughout the 1980s, especially after General Manuel Antonio Noriega assumed command of the military, which is now designated as the Panamanian Defense Force (PDF). Noriega engineered the 1984 election of President Nicolas Ardito Barletta, and then removed him the following year when Barletta supported an investigation into the murder of a prominent Noriega critic. In 1987 accusations made against Noriega by a forcibly retired PDF officer, Colonel Roberto Diaz Herrera, led to widespread rioting and increased repression. In 1988, after the general's indictment in Florida on charges involving narcotics smuggling, the Reagan administration began a concerted effort to replace Noriega. These efforts failed as Noriega again ousted the incumbent president and installed another puppet in his place. When, despite continuing repression, the political opposition coalition managed to win the 1989 presidential elections, Noriega simply annulled the results. U.S. pressures and capital flight devastated the nation's economy, but the general managed to hang on until a full-scale U.S. invasion forced him from power in December. The invasion decapitated the PDF; most high-ranking officers were either arrested or forced into retirement.[25]

The newly installed government of President Guillermo Endara faced a major problem in coping with the remnants of the defeated PDF. Riddled by corruption, despised by much of the population, and bitter over the opposition's cooperation in the invasion, the force had no loyalty to the new administration. Because the PDF was the nation's only police force, however, its total elimination would have compelled U.S. forces to undertake that task for a prolonged period— a contingency that was clearly unacceptable to the U.S. military or the Bush administration. As a result, a new Public Force, composed primarily of members of the old PDF, was created. The Public Force had sharply reduced authority and military components, which produced some criticism from those who thought that this force was inadequate, and considerably more criticism from those who feared that it would be the predecessor of a resurrected PDF. This issue has become

25. For descriptions of these events see Frederick Kempe, *Divorcing the Dictator* (Putnam, 1990).

extremely divisive within Panama, and the wave of criticism has been demoralizing to those commanding the force.[26]

ANALYSIS AND PROJECTIONS

Although the traditional pattern of civil-military relations in Central America has deteriorated during the past decade, many components of that pattern continue to exist. The officers are still a separate caste. Concerned more about institutional survival than anything else, they are suspicious of both domestic and foreign politicians, and are determined to defend their powers and privileges at almost any cost. Civilians remain alienated from, and often contemptuous of, the military, but frequently prefer to involve the military in politics rather than relinquish power to their civilian opponents. Although both groups proclaim their commitment to democracy and human rights, it is difficult to evaluate either the depth or the sincerity of such commitments.

Some factors appear common to Honduras, Guatemala, and El Salvador. Although the military has expanded greatly in each nation during the past decade, the repeatedly predicted militarization of the societies may not be occurring. Military power has increased, and the concept of mission has expanded, but the relative institutional advantage that the armed forces have long held over other sectors of society has actually diminished. Political parties, labor groups, private-sector organizations, and religious bodies have developed external ties that rival those of the military. At the same time, urbanization and the revolution in mass communications have made it impossible to exercise the degree of control over information, organization, and political action that was possible forty years ago. The increasing complexity of Central American societies has made effective control of the political process impossible for any single group, class, or institution.

There is a regionwide trend toward an increasing unwillingness of the armed forces to commit themselves to any single political or economic faction. The extreme Right is often trusted little more than the political Left. Similar to a Brazilian general in 1950, Central American officers have come to dislike and distrust "the maleficent embittered

26. FBIS, May 22, 1990, p. 31.

forces of passion, of parties, and of all the uncontrolled ambitions of individuals and . . . dissatisfied interest groups."[27] This distrust extends to individual officers as well as to civilians. It is worth noting that since 1981, generals Garcia and Blandon in El Salvador, Lucas and Rios Montt in Guatemala, and Alvarez and Lopez in Honduras have all been ejected from positions of power by their fellow officers.

Civil-military relations have improved to some degree in each nation over the past decade, but the pattern has been uneven. In El Salvador the most important changes occurred from 1983 until 1986. Since then, there has been little progress, and there are even signs of reversal. The resolution of the Jesuit murders will be a key indication of whether progress will resume or whether the situation will continue to deteriorate. In Guatemala, however, the pattern of change began in 1982, and, although the entire process remains extremely fragile, the greatest changes may have occurred since 1985. The May 1990 retirement of General Gramajo as defense minister, combined with recent increases in human rights violations, cast doubt upon the continuation or even maintenance of this progress, however. In Honduras, neither human rights abuses, nor the unbridled exercise of military power, had approached the levels of the other two nations. By the same token, although civilian government seems solidly in place, the amount of actual change there is probably less than for its neighbors, and the pattern of civil-military relations has shown little change over the past three years. Recently installed President Rafael Leonardo Callejas appears to be potentially able to exert increased civilian authority over the military, but whether he will ultimately summon either the will or the power to do so is questionable.

The prevailing situations in Nicaragua and Panama present unique problems. In the short run, prospects for enhanced civilian authority seem best in Panama, but problems in the area of civil-military relations remain formidable for both governments.

One obvious manifestation of change is that armies no longer find it desirable to overthrow governments. They are, however, increasingly tempted to eject rivals within the military establishment. Some elements, especially in Guatemala, still advocate coups, but it has become almost impossible to unite the military behind such adventures.

Human rights remain a major problem. Political and military con-

27. Cited in Robert Wesson, *Democracy in Latin America: Promise and Problems* (Praeger, 1982), pp. 157–158.

siderations appear to instigate any improvements that occur in this area. Many officers resent what they consider external infringements upon their capacity to eliminate their enemies. A Salvadoran Air Force officer, complaining about the restrictions placed upon bombing operations by U.S. advisers, suggested that the Salvadoran Air Force should be free to use the same tactics to defeat the guerrillas that the United States used to defeat Germany and Japan, thereby equating Salvadoran civilians in guerrilla-held areas with Germans in Dresden and Japanese in Hiroshima.[28]

The future course of civil-military relations will depend upon a number of factors. A key factor will be the economy. Prolonged economic stagnation or further decline will undermine the prospects for democracy, increase domestic turmoil, discredit existing governments, and increase support for a possible coup. Assuming responsibility for a failing economy, however, will not be an attractive prospect for many officers. The most likely impact of such a scenario is further confusion, conflict, and division, which will prevent the creation of any stable pattern of civil-military relations.

The increasing economic involvement and power of officers is a real threat to any improvement in civil-military relations. Such involvement influenced the decision by Nicaragua's middle and upper classes to withdraw support from the Somozas and significantly affected the recent turmoil in Panama.

The course of insurgencies, especially in El Salvador and Guatemala, is a major factor in the future evolution of civil-military relations. Prospects appear dim for any quick settlement. A slow resolution of these conflicts might permit a strengthening of civil institutions and a reduction in the scope of power exercised by the military. Conversely, any major escalation could reduce the discretion permitted civilian politicians and produce a rapid resurgence in human rights abuses.

Negotiations with insurgents in El Salvador and Guatemala could disrupt civil-military relations. The danger is less in El Salvador under the ARENA government than it was previously, but it still exists. Although many officers in El Salvador and Guatemala now recognize the necessity of a political, rather than a military, solution to their conflicts, they remain extremely suspicious of negotiations with insur-

28. Interview with Salvadoran Air Force major, 1985.

gents and are determined not to permit such forces to keep their arms or to control any territory.

In Nicaragua it now appears that the contras will largely disarm, which will reduce the danger their presence poses for civil-military relations. The enmity between the contras and the military, however, will be a continuous problem—one that could be significantly aggravated if the military begins to believe that the contras are being given preferential treatment by the Chamorro government.

An end to current conflicts would not necessarily lead to better civil-military relations. A study by four U.S. Army lieutenant colonels concluded that, after the current conflict ends, Salvador's military

> is likely to become a drag on efforts to restore healthy internal development and may also complicate American efforts to create regional stability . . . . Given its history, a muscular, assertive Salvadoran military is unlikely to accept a backrow seat in Salvadoran politics unless the officer corps receives appropriate inducements to do so. If anything . . . education in modern warfare—blurring the line between the military and non-military realms—may create new incentives to remain in politics as officers extend the parameters of national security beyond traditional combat against an armed adversary.[29]

Narcotics, especially in Honduras, could potentially both disrupt civil-military relations and produce conflicts within the armed forces. Competing factions within the officer corps of Honduras and Guatemala have already begun to accuse their opponents of involvement with narcotics, hoping thereby to gain U.S. support for their faction, or, at the least, end Washington's support for their opponents. The narcotics issue is likely to become increasingly important in coming years.

The final factor—one that is most difficult to predict—that will shape civil-military relations will be the assumption of power, in the 1990s, by officers who directly experienced the violence of the 1980s. In Panama, where that violence resulted in the installation of the current government, this could be a special problem.

The next generation of officers will be better educated, and more exposed to psychological operations, problems of national develop-

29. Bacevich and others, "American Military Policy," pp. 87–88.

ment, and alternative models of politics. They already show signs of increasing frustration with traditional approaches, both military and civilian, to major national issues. They are unlikely to identify with any particular civilian political sector, and are less likely than their predecessors to place heavy reliance for institutional survival on external forces. They will be more nationalistic, more independent, and more skeptical, but no more willing to place their ultimate fate in civilian hands. They may also be more fractionated, raising the risk of open conflicts within the military. What pattern of civil-military relations will ultimately emerge with such officers commanding the armed forces is impossible to predict, but it will not be a return to the pre-1979 pattern.

CONCLUSIONS

Traditional formulas and prognostications concerning the nature and course of civil-military relations in Central America are rapidly becoming outdated. Among both civilians and officers, there is a growing realization that not only are previous patterns undesirable, they are also threatening to the interests of all concerned. Neither civilians nor officers are independently able to maintain internal security, nor to deal with their nations' staggering social and economic problems. Neither group is satisfied with the current status of relations; neither is willing to concede basic authority to the other. No new consensus on civil-military relations has emerged, nor is one likely to emerge in the near future.

The ability to understand and evaluate the changes taking place is hampered by ignorance of the actual respective attitudes toward the issue. Much work remains to be done in this area. It seems unlikely that Guatemala, Honduras, or El Salvador will approach the level of accommodation in civil-military relations that has characterized Venezuela for the past quarter of a century, but it also seems unlikely, though not impossible, that they will slide into the disastrous confrontational model that existed in Panama prior to the December 1989 invasion. In Nicaragua tensions between government and military are likely to be constant throughout the Chamorro administration. In Panama the new Public Force has little choice in the immediate future other than to accept civilian control, but ingrained resentment over the invasion, class and racial divisions, and the continuing heritage of the PDF within the officer corps, presents a very real possibility for confrontation in the more distant future.

Throughout the region, what seems most likely to occur is a period of prolonged uncertainty, conflict, and division. Such a time, although unsatisfactory to all concerned, could produce a slow, uneven, and fragile move toward greater political freedom for civilians, continued internal autonomy for the military, and a very slow and painful improvement in human rights conditions. Numerous factors—economic, political, and military—could upset this scenario, but, of the myriad possible outcomes by the end of the century, this appears the most probable.

Conference Participants

with their affiliations at the time of the conference

Ernesto Altschul
Vice Minister of the Presidency,
El Salvador

Sergio Alvarez
Caribbean Central American Action

Walter Arsenberg
World Resources Institute

Bernard Aronson
U.S. Department of State

Cynthia Arnson
Americas Watch

John Bailey
Georgetown University

William M. Barbieri
Inter-American Foundation

Adolfo Blandon
Embassy of El Salvador

Louis W. Cabot
Brookings Institution

Maryellen Cabot
Brookings Institution

Ricardo Castaneda
Ambassador of El Salvador to
the United Nations

Ricardo Chavira
Time

Charles Ciccolella
The Army-Air Force Center for
Low Intensity Conflict

Isaac Cohen
Economic Commission for Latin
America and the Caribbean

William S. Cohen
U.S. Senate

Forrest Colburn
Princeton University

Nancy Cook
World Bank

Peter Copeland
Scripps-Howard

Melvyn R. Copen
Instituto Centroamericano de
Administracion de Empresas

Ben Crosby
Overseas Development Council/INCAE

Silvio de Franco
Minister of Economy and Development
Nicaragua

Melinda De Lashmutt
International Center for Development
Policy

Francisco R.R. de Sola
De Sola, S.A.

John Dingus
National Public Radio

Martha Doggett
Lawyers Committee for Human Rights

James Dorsey
Washington Times

Luigi R. Einaudi
U.S. Department of State

Tom Farer
American University

Richard Feinberg
Overseas Development Council

Patrick Flynn
Journalist

Nancy S. Gillespie
World Bank

Guadalupe Gonzalez
Political Diplomatic Commission,
FDR and FMLM
El Salvador

Richard Gonzalez
National Public Radio

William Goodfellow
Center for International Policy

Robert Greenberger
Wall Street Journal

Joseph Grunwald
University of California, San Diego

Tom Hart
Brookings Institution

Margaret D. Hayes
Inter-American Development Bank

Larry Heilman
MSI

David Holiday
Washington Office on Latin America

Peter B. Johnson
Central American Action

Joseph Jova
Van Kloberg Associates

James Kaesel
Arlington, Va.

Erik Kjonnerod
National Defense University

Lawrence Korb
Brookings Institution

Alexander A. Kravetz
Mission of El Salvador

Robert J. Kurz
Brookings Institution

William Leogrande
American University

Nancy Llach
Washington, D.C.

Nora C. Lustig
Brookings Institution

Bruce K. MacLaury
Brookings Institution

Juan Vincente Maldonado
FUSADES

Sergio Mantamoras
BAO, Inc.

Bennett Marsh
Caribbean Central American Action

Jessica L. Masten
Brookings Institution

Francisco Mayorga
Central Bank of Nicaragua

Dick McCall
Office of Senator John F. Kerry

Donald F. McHenry
Georgetown University

Martin McReynolds
Miami Herald

James H. Michel
Agency for International Development

Richard Millett
Southern Illinois University

Tommy Sue Montgomery
Agnes Scott College

James Morrell
Washington Office on Latin America

Roberto Murray-Meza
La Constancia, S.A.

Arthur M. Niner, Jr.
Greyman International Inc.

April Olivier
MacNeil/Lehrer Newshour

George Park
World Bank

Norma Parker
U.S. Department of State

Robert Pastor
The Carter Center of Emory University

Susan Kaufman Purcell
The Americas Society

Julio Sergio Ramirez
INCAE

Julie Rauner
U.S. Department of Commerce

Charles A. Reilly
Inter-American Foundation

Mark Rosenberg
Florida International University

Randolph Ryan
Boston Globe

Miguel Angel Salaverria
*Ambassador from El Salvador
to the United States*

Randy Scheunemann
House Foreign Affairs Committee

Mike Sheehan
National Security Council

Janet Shenk
Arca Foundation

· Barry Sklar
Senate Foreign Relations Committee

Bruce L. R. Smith
Brookings Institution

Gare Smith
Office of Senator Edward M. Kennedy

Robert Stark
*Policy Alternatives for the
Caribbean and Central America*

John D. Steinbruner
Brookings Institution

Elena Suarez
Caribbean Central American Action

Deborah Szekely
Inter-American Foundation

Arturo Valenzuela
Georgetown University

Eduardo Vallarino
*Ambassador of Panama to the
United States*

Francesc Vendrell
United Nations

Stephen Vetter
Inter-American Foundation

Juan Walte
USA Today

Robert White
*International Center for
Development Policy*

Alexander Wilde
Washington Office on Latin America

Murat Williams
Washington, D.C.

Susan K. Williams
Brookings Institution

Ruben Zamora
*Popular Social Christian Movement,
El Salvador*